FRONTLINE MADRID

FRONTLINE MADRID

Battlefield Tours of the Spanish Civil War

David Mathieson

An imprint of Interlink Publishing Group, Inc.
Northampton, Massachusetts

First published in 2016 by
INTERLINK BOOKS
An imprint of Interlink Publishing Group, Inc.
46 Crosby Street, Northampton, Massachusetts 01060
www.interlinkbooks.com

Published simultaneously in the United Kingdom by Signal Books, Oxford

Library of Congress Cataloging-in-Publication Data

Mathieson, David, 1960 July 24-
Frontline Madrid : battlefield tours of the Spanish Civil War / by David Mathieson.
pages cm
Includes bibliographical references and index.
ISBN 978-1-56656-086-3
1. Battlefields--Spain--Madrid--Guidebooks. 2. Historic sites--Spain--Madrid (Region)--Guidebooks. 3. Madrid (Spain)--History--Siege, 1936-1939. 4. Spain--History--Civil War, 1936-1939--Battlefields--Guidebooks. 5. Madrid (Spain)--Tours. I. Title.
DP269.27.M3M38 2015
946.081'4094641--dc23
2015014308

Cover Design: Baseline Arts, Oxford
Typesetting: Tora Kelly
Cover Images: © David Mathieson; James Ferguson; courtesy Wikimedia Commons
Half-title page: Marching off to war: Republican solders on the Brunete front, 1937 (Ministerio de Educación, Cultura y Deporte, Archivo General de la Administración (Archivo Rojo))

Printed and bound in the United States of America

CONTENTS

Foreword by Jon Snow vii

1 The Spanish Civil War and Siege of Madrid 1

2 A Quick Guide to the International Brigades in 20 Questions and Answers 17

3 20 Spanish Civil War Sites in Madrid City Center: A Quick Guide 31

4 The Massacre at the Montaña Barracks 60

5 Madrid's Western Front: The Casa de Campo, Parque del Oeste, and University Campus 76

6 The Battle of Jarama: General Franco's Plan C 112

7 Hemingway's War: Guadarrama, Valle de los Caídos, and El Escorial 150

8 The Battle of Brunete: If Not Here, Then Where? 185

Delving Deeper: Top Ten Books, Top Ten Websites 224

Acknowledgments 231

Index 234

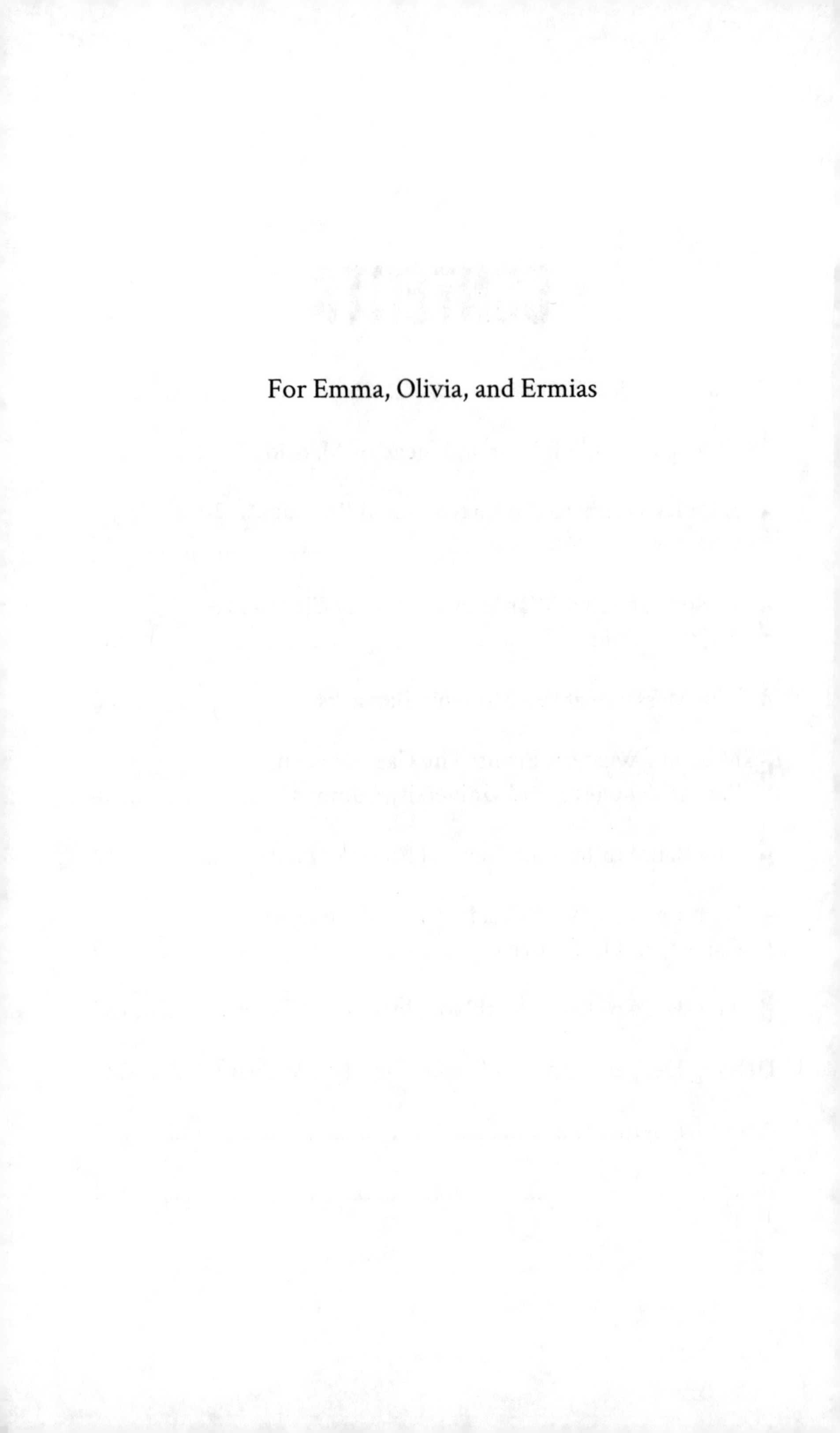

For Emma, Olivia, and Ermias

FOREWORD BY JON SNOW

It is now nearly eighty years since the outbreak of the Spanish Civil War, which savaged much of the country between 1936 and 1939. The conflict had dire consequences for many Spaniards but its repercussions went far beyond the Iberian Peninsula and marked a watershed in twentieth-century European history. It was in Spain that the juggernaut of European fascism in the 1930s met its first serious resistance when the elected Republican government fought to prevent a military takeover led by General Franco. Before 1936 Hitler and Mussolini had muscled their way to victory from Abyssinia to the Rhineland. After Spain the dictators had to face the full force of the Allies who confronted them from 1939 onwards in World War II.

The struggle for control of Madrid—the subject of this timely and original book—was central to the resistance of totalitarianism in Spain. For nearly three years ordinary *Madrileños* defended their city against the siege laid by Franco's troops under the slogan "No Pasarán" (they shall not pass). That slogan has remained an inspiration to anti-fascists ever since: I have seen it repeated time and again when reporting from Latin America and elsewhere by popular movements standing up against authoritarian regimes.

And, despite the passage of time, the war in Spain remains a reference point in other ways too. In 1936 the elected Republican government in Spain was cold-shouldered by other democracies such as Britain, France, and the USA, which were intent on appeasing the rising tide of European fascism. We now know (as many did even then) that the policy was a calamitous mistake. Yet the questions of when, where, and how to intervene effectively to reign in authoritarian governments or prevent humanitarian catastrophes are among the most important issues of our age; in that debate the war in Spain is frequently cited as an example of how to deal with—or how not to deal with—international crises.

The deficit left by the failure of the political establishment to help the Spanish Republic was met in part at least by the International Brigades. These volunteers from over fifty different countries saw clearly, even if many of their myopic governments did not, that totalitarian aggression had to be fought. *Frontline Madrid* now provides an invaluable guide to the battlefield sites in and around Madrid where, alongside ordinary Spaniards, the volunteers of the IB were prepared to put their lives on the line.

In the winter of 1936 Geoffrey Cox, a young journalist who later went on to become Editor here at ITN, wrote from Madrid: "whatever the future brings, the defense of Madrid in these days remains, in the face of terrible odds, one of the finest chapters in the history of the common people of the world."

This book tells their incredible story.

1

THE SPANISH CIVIL WAR AND SIEGE OF MADRID

A BACKGROUND GUIDE IN 20 QUESTIONS AND ANSWERS

1. WHEN WAS THE SPANISH CIVIL WAR?

The Spanish Civil War started on the evening of the 17 July 1936. It ended nearly three years later on 1 April 1939 when rebel troops known as Nationalists finally defeated forces loyal to the Republican government.

2. DID PEOPLE SEE THE WAR COMING?

Not really. On 17 July some officers of the Spanish military high command declared a *coup d'état* to overthrow the democratically elected Republican government in Madrid. Army interventions, known as *pronunciamentos,* were not uncommon in Spanish political history. Between 1820 and 1923 there were over forty *pronunciamentos* and for most of the 1920s Spain had been ruled by a military dictator, General Miguel Primo de Rivera. Few were surprised when the army tried t]o intervene in 1936 but both sides underestimated the other: government ministers were slow to react because they did not believe the plotters had sufficient support, while the rebels failed to gauge popular enthusiasm for the Republic. Moreover, Spain had kept out of World War I so there was no mass experience of industrial-scale warfare. Many people were at best semi-literate and had read nothing about the horrors of the Western Front. As a consequence there was little comprehension of the implications of the war about to be unleashed—a conflict which would last nearly three years and leave up to half a million Spaniards dead.

3. SO WHY WAS IT DIFFERENT THIS TIME?

Instead of the swift regime change which the military expected, the *coup* was botched. Troops in seven of Spain's nine biggest cities remained loyal to the Republic. The elected government had several faults but many Spaniards thought that the alternative—some form of rightwing dictatorship—would be far worse. Crucially, there was popular support for the Republican government in Spain's two most important cities, Madrid and Barcelona. The rebels' plan A was to topple the Republic by a *coup*. When that failed they were forced to embark on plan B—a military campaign to take control of the country and the government by force. Within days the Italian fascist leader Benito Mussolini and the Nazi Führer Adolf Hitler sent troops and supplies to sustain the uprising. And so the Civil War began.

4. WHAT WERE THE TWO SIDES FIGHTING ABOUT?

The soul of Spain—or to put it another way, almost everything. A popular explanation even today of Spanish history is the theory of the "Two Spains." On the one side were deeply conservative forces: the monarchy and nobles, the military, the Catholic Church, the large landowners, and, to a lesser extent, industrialists in the north. On countless occasions these traditionally powerful groups resisted even modest reforms which threatened their privileges. A popular refrain insisted that "half of Spain works but does not eat while the other half eats but does not work." The army, for example, consisted of a 12,000-strong officer corps (including over 200 generals) which commanded some 160,000 troops held in garrison towns all over Spain. Yet there was no external threat to Spain and only the vestiges of empire—the one remaining colony in Morocco—to protect. As the military historian Antony Beevor comments, "this over manned and incompetent organization was a heavy charge on the state. Its role was never clear." The Catholic Church was another large predatory body which effectively formed a state within the state. Although the notorious Spanish Inquisition was officially wound up in the nineteenth century, a culture of intolerant religious zealotry lived on. An additional, fanatical input to the Spanish right was provided by the Falange movement, founded in 1933, which deliberately aped Italian fascism. General Franco, the leader of the Nationalist uprising, often claimed that he was at the head of a "crusade" against godless Marxism, but others thought that any such crusade was really about resisting modernity and the ideas of the Enlightenment. Eugenio Vegas Latapié, a rightwing, monarchist intellectual, said bluntly: "in 1936 we were fighting against the influence of French Revolutionary ideas."

On the other side, however, radicalism was also a prominent feature of Spanish politics: the country had one of the largest anarchist movements in Europe, one of the oldest socialist parties in the world, and an avant-garde cultural elite which included artists like Luis Buñuel, Salvador Dalí, and Picasso. The radicals were frequently hell-bent on sweeping away all that had gone before. Moderate voices were few amidst the intransigence and there was little common ground. Both sides in the Civil War were diverse coalitions with internal disagreements but what united them was a visceral hatred of *el otro bando*—the other lot. Looking back on the social tensions of the 1930s and the causes of the conflict, Ramón Serrano Suñer, General Franco's brother-in-law and chief adviser, commented simply, "the truth is, we Spaniards couldn't stand each other."

Republican Government propaganda depicting the Nationalist coalition: the Church, the military, a Nazi-sympathizing financier, and Moorish mercenaries. (Bibliothèque Nationale, Paris)

5. HOW DID THESE DIFFERENCES COME TO A HEAD IN THE 1930S?

In 1929 the Wall Street crash triggered a global economic crisis which, in turn, exacerbated an economic and political crisis in Spain. In 1930 the military dictator General Primo de Rivera was ousted by his army colleagues. In April 1931 the ineffectual and unpopular King Alfonso XIII also fled. This left a power vacuum from which the Second Republic was born (the First Republic was a short-lived affair in the 1870s). The new government hit a series of problems from the start. Unemployment soared and there was no social security system to cushion the hardship. Nationalists in regions like Catalonia demanded more autonomy. The left expected rapid, radical reforms across the board and the government passed new laws to improve working conditions, redistribute land, reduce the privileges of the Church, improve education, and modernize the army. But many of these measures were frequently thwarted by the powerful and wealthy upper class, and in any event they failed to meet the pent-up expectations of the workers. The right, on the other hand, resisted any change whatsoever. Several of the tepid reforms were less threatening than they seemed but many of the groups challenged—the army, Church, and landowners—were scared by the fiery rhetoric of some leftwing politicians. It was a disastrous combination. The Republican government was increasingly regarded by the radical left as one which routinely over-promised and under-delivered, while the right became convinced that Spain was about to disintegrate in an anarchist-communist-socialist revolution.

6. SO THE SECOND REPUBLIC WAS UNSTABLE?

Yes, from the outset. Between 1931 and 1936 control of the Republic swung between left and right with little resistance in the middle. Democratic culture was weak. Just a year after the Republic was born some army officers led by General José Sanjurjo attempted a military *coup* which became known as the *sanjurada*. The plot failed but when the right came to power in elections in 1933 the left immediately declared a general strike to cripple the new government. In between, both leftist and rightwing governments used the paramilitary Guardia Civil to stamp on local dissent. Many innocent lives were lost. In 1934, for example, a strike by Asturian miners was put down with particular ferocity by troops under the command of one General Franco. It was estimated that around 2,000 workers were killed or executed. In some cities like Barcelona and Madrid there were waves of anti-clerical burnings of churches and other properties. When a coalition of leftwing groups known as the Popular Front won the parliamentary elections in February 1936, army officers began to plot another coup and the Falange (fascist) movement stepped up its campaign of political assassinations. The communists, anarchists, and socialists responded in kind. By early summer dozens of people were being taken every week for a *paseo* (a walk from which there was no return), victims of the tit-for-tat killings. In a bid to avoid more trouble the government deliberately stationed the most hostile generals well away from Madrid, but behind the scenes senior military commanders now began plotting to overthrow the Republic.

7. WHAT WAS THE FINAL STRAW?

On the evening of 12 July 1936 Jose del Castillo, an officer in the Assault Guards (a security force loyal to the Republic), was walking to work down the Calle Fuencarral in the center of Madrid. Castillo never reached his destination because he was gunned down in the street by Falangist assassins. His enraged colleagues sought revenge. In the early hours of the following morning they went to the apartment of José Calvo Sotelo, leader of a monarchist group in the parliament and well known for his inflammatory, left-baiting speeches. They told the politician that he was wanted for police questioning—an unlikely proposition given that he enjoyed parliamentary immunity from arrest under the constitution. Calvo Sotelo promised his wife and children that he would return soon "unless these gentlemen blow my brains out." As they drove down the Calle de Velázquez that is exactly what the Assault Guards did. The corpse was then dumped outside the city's East Cemetery. Although it had been planned well in advance, the murder of Calvo Sotelo was the excuse the military conspirators need for their attempted *coup*. On 17 July generals in various garrison towns around Spain led revolts against the civilian authorities. The attempted uprising in Madrid itself, however, was a failure. What happened at the Montaña Barracks is the subject of Chapter 4.

8. WHAT WAS GENERAL FRANCO'S ROLE IN THE *COUP* ATTEMPT?

In July 1936 Francisco Franco was just one of several generals closely involved in the plot against the Republic. The youngest general in the Spanish army and known for his rightwing views, Franco was something of a national hero because of his leadership of Spain's Army of Africa which suppressed revolts among nationalist Moroccan tribesmen during the 1920s. Many of the other generals were more senior than 43-year-old Franco though, and initially it was not even certain that the inscrutable young officer would join the rebellion at all. The Republican government, however, never trusted Franco and had sent him to the Canary Islands in a deliberate ploy to keep him away from the Spanish mainland. But in a murky operation involving Britain's MI6 he was airlifted to Morocco where he rejoined his beloved Army of Africa. Within weeks of the uprising, Franco's stock grew ever higher as the more senior ringleaders died in accidents or were captured by the Republicans. Other rivals were quietly but effectively outmanoeuvred by the crafty Franco. On 21 September 1936 he was named as *caudillo* or total commander of the Nationalist forces—military and civilian. It was the start of nearly four decades of dictatorial rule based on the cult of his personality, yet few ever actually got to know him beyond the propaganda images and slogans. His personal chaplain for over forty years summed up the enigma when he said of Franco, "perhaps he was as cold as some have said but he never showed it. In fact, he never showed anything."

9. DID OTHER COUNTRIES GET INVOLVED IN THE CONFLICT?

Yes—several, although many promised not to. During the summer and autumn of 1936 world attention focused on Spain and the conflict threatened to destabilize the fragile European order. The liberal democracies (Britain, France, and the USA) made a messy agreement with the Axis powers of European fascism (Germany and Italy) and Stalin's Soviet Union not to become involved. This was called the Non-Intervention Agreement. None of the dictators kept their word but the liberal democracies did nothing to back up the agreement—Winston Churchill derided the whole thing as "an elaborate system of official humbug." Mussolini sent over 80,000 troops and Hitler some 35,000 Germans—including the notorious Condor Legion—to aid the Nationalists. Stalin sent advisors, tanks, aircraft, and ordnance to the Republicans. As a result, one German general described Spain as being akin to a "European Aldershot" where different countries trained key service personnel and experimented with new battlefront techniques.

One of the most important groups of all, however, were 80,000 ruthless mercenaries from the Spanish protectorate of Morocco who fought with the Nationalists. When the Republican airforce bombed the Moroccan port of Tetuán to prevent its use by rebel troops, innocent civilians were killed. Not surprisingly, this inflamed opinion on the streets and turned ordinary Moroccans against the Republic. Along with bribes and false promises of independence for the protectorate from Franco, these actions led to thousands of Moroccan fighters—good Muslims to a man—joining the Nationalists' Catholic crusade against the Republic.

On the other side some 45,000 or so volunteers from 50 different countries—including Britain, Ireland, and the United States—went to fight for the Republic. The volunteers formed what were known as the International Brigades and they played a key role in all the battles described in this book. Their contribution is explored in Chapter 2.

10. Why was the siege of Madrid so important in the conflict?

To quote Napoleon, "just look at the map!" Slap bang in the center of Spain, the capital was the seat of the government. One Republican commander, Vicente Rojo, said that for Nationalists and Republicans alike Madrid presented an objective which was "precise, categoric, and well defined." He argued that there are few examples in the history of warfare in which control of a target—"strategic and tactical, political and social, economic and geographic"—meant so much to both sides. The fate of the besieged city captured world attention and its most important landmarks during this time are explored in Chapter 3.

11. When did the Nationalists reach Madrid?

Once it became apparent that the *coup* had failed, the rebel generals realized that Madrid would need to be taken by force. By 6 November 1936 columns of the Nationalist army reached the outskirts of the capital, confident that the city would quickly fall. One hubristic Nationalist radio broadcast precipitously described Franco entering the Puerto del Sol in the center of the city on a white horse. By 8 November the Nationalist army began to take control of large sections of the huge parkland known as the Casa de Campo on the western side of the city. The Casa de Campo had for centuries been preserved as hunting grounds for the king, and fans out from the Royal Palace in the center of Madrid towards the mountains in the north and west. As a consequence, Nationalist forces were able to get very close to the city before they met serious Republican resistance.

12. WHO LED THE ATTACK AND WHO LED THE DEFENSE?

General Franco did not personally lead the attack on Madrid. This task was given to General José Enrique Varela, one of Franco's closest associates who commanded the Nationalist 7th Division. Like Franco, Varela was a veteran of the wars against the Rif tribes in Morocco. Short in stature and irascible by nature, Varela liked to wear white kid gloves into battle—although he did not treat prisoners with kid gloves. His army was a mixture of Moroccan mercenaries and Spanish Legionnaires. All were seasoned, professional fighters, ruthless, well equipped, and disciplined under a unitary command.

The civilian politicians fled Madrid in early November to establish a new seat of government in Valencia for the duration of the war. The defense of the capital was left in the hands of a *junta* (council) led by General José Miaja and his highly capable second-in-command, Colonel Vicente Rojo. Both were regular army officers who remained loyal to the Republic, but many under their command were civilians organized into militia. These *ad hoc* groups had different political affiliations—communist, socialist, Trotskyist, and anarchist—and were often suspicious of each other and unaccustomed to military discipline of any kind. To make matters worse, the weapons and equipment supplied to the militia were frequently of poor quality—or simply non-existent.

13. WHAT WAS THE NATIONALIST PLAN OF ATTACK?

In the assault on Madrid the Nationalist army was split into four columns. One column held the line to the north of the city to stem any possible counterattack from the Republican forces gathered there. The other three columns advanced though the Casa de Campo and attacked Madrid from its western flank at various points along the Manzanares river. This covered a stretch of roughly one kilometer from the university district to the Plaza de España. The Nationalists also boasted about the existence of a "fifth column"—sympathizers already inside the city ready to rise up and sabotage the defense effort when given the signal (the expression "fifth columnist" is still used today to describe potential traitors). General Varela—and most observers—expected a quick Nationalist victory.

14. WHAT WERE THE PROBLEMS WITH THE NATIONALIST PLAN?

The Nationalists' plan underestimated the peculiar topography of Madrid which complicated the plan of attack. First, it entailed crossing the River Manzanares. This was expected to be more of an inconvenience than a real challenge since the river (now canalized) was neither especially wide nor deep. The lack of a navigable waterway to the sea helps explain Madrid's comparatively poor economic development through the centuries and the Manzanares has been the butt of several jokes. The French author Victor Hugo ordered a glass of water with a meal while visiting Madrid. He left half and told the waiter to pour what was left into the Manzanares, quipping that the river evidently needed it more than he did. Napoleon took one look and commented that Madrid either needed to get a new river or take away some of the bridges as it evidently did not need both. Nevertheless, getting across the Manzares under sustained fire proved to be a lethal exercise.

The Manzanares River has been mocked throughout history but played a crucial role in the defense of Madrid. Republican lines along the river held, forcing the Nationalists to abandon their original plan of attack. (Manuel M. Vicente/Wikimedia Commons)

Second, the western part of Madrid is on an escarpment which rises abruptly from the river bank through what was even then the ornamental Parque del Oeste. Although the park has since been re-landscaped the topography remains the same and the slopes are steep. Today it is still easy to imagine the difficulty mounting an attack on the rising ground. There were profound disagreements among the Nationalist commanders about the planned assault. Some thought that attacking the city across a river and up an escarpment was just too risky—even if the defenses were not thought to be particularly robust. What happened during the battle through the Parque del Oeste and university campus is the subject of Chapter 5.

15. Why didn't the Nationalists try a different approach?

The problem for Franco and Varela was that all the alternatives to attacking Madrid from the west looked worse. General Mola's Nationalist army had intended to enter Madrid from the north but could advance no further than the Sierra de Guadarrama, about 45 kilometers directly north of the city. These mountains extend around the northwest of Madrid like a natural shield and have protected the city for centuries. Mola's army was pinned down by determined Republican resistance. With the onset of the bitter winter which brings heavy snow falls to block the passes, there was no expectation that they would break through for months—if at all. The Sierra de Guadarrama provided the backdrop to Hemingway's classic novel about the war, *For Whom the Bell Tolls*. What happened in the mountains is discussed in Chapter 7.

Taking the city from the south would have involved house to house fighting through districts like Carabanchel, Usera, and La Latina. These poor *barrios* (districts) formed the "red belt" where most people were highly sympathetic to the Republicans—a local leader claimed that there would have been "a rifle at every window"—and the professional soldiers of Franco's army wanted to avoid fighting urban guerrilla warfare. So despite the evident risks, there was only one real choice open to the Nationalists in the first week of November 1936. To take Madrid they needed to attack from the west, through the open ground of the Casa de Campo and Parque del Oeste.

Having failed to take Madrid in a direct military *coup* or by weeks of siege, the Nationalist commanders tried yet another approach in February 1937. This time they attempted to conquer Madrid from the east through the valley of the Jarama river (see Chapter 6).

16. WERE THE REPUBLICANS WELL PREPARED?

To a degree. Although the defense of Madrid relied largely on a rag-bag of untrained civilian militias, they were helped by luck and poor Nationalist tactics. In the early autumn of 1936 General Franco diverted troops to break the Republican siege of Toledo, the one-time capital of Spain. To the frustration of the German military advisors, the attack delayed the much more important assault on Madrid by around six weeks. In terms of military strategy it was a quixotic decision (in every sense) which gave the Republicans crucial time in which to import more weapons and better organize the defense of the capital. Republican commanders calculated that the rebels would try to take Madrid from the western side and by a stroke of luck they soon found out precisely where the attack would be launched. A Nationalist armored car was blown up in fierce fighting as the rebels closed in on the city and the body search of a dead Italian officer inside revealed top secret battle plans for the final attack on the city center. The Republicans now knew where the Nationalists intended to strike and how. Armed with this vital new intelligence, the Republicans dug in and the siege of Madrid began.

17. HOW MANY PEOPLE WERE INVOLVED?

In total around 1.8 million men fought on the Republican side and 1.4 million enlisted with the Nationalist army during the course of the war. Around 20,000 Nationalist troops laid siege to Madrid in November 1936 while some 30,000 Republican troops and militia were involved in the defense of the city. (The population of Spain at the time was around 25 million, with one million people living in Madrid.)

18. Why didn't the Republicans counterattack?

They did—but without success. In the summer of 1937 the Republicans began a huge offensive which tried to break the Nationalist supply lines between Madrid and the west of Spain. The attack focused on some of the villages around Brunete—a point on the frontline around 40 kilometers from Madrid's center (see Chapter 8).

19. How long did the siege of Madrid last?

Madrid resisted the Nationalist siege until the end of the Civil War. By then much of Spain had fallen into Nationalist hands and the Republic was broken. Morale amongst the starving population of Madrid collapsed and on 1 April 1939 Franco's victorious troops entered the city unopposed.

20. How did the conflict end?

Badly. By the end, parts of Madrid were in ruins and thousands were starving. The political rivalries which had bedeviled the Republic from the outset came to the fore once again. Communists, socialists, and anarchists set on each other and seemed more intent on settling old scores rather than fighting the Nationalists—it was a civil war within a civil war. Those who could got out. More than half a million Spaniards fled over the Pyrenees to France and exile. When France itself was invaded a few months later by Germany, some joined the *maquis*—the French Resistance. Thousands of others, including the former Prime Minister of the Republic, Largo Caballero—were passed on to Nazi concentration camps. Of those who stayed, tens of thousands more were subjected to Franco's vicious repression. The merciless persecution of Republicans continued well into the 1940s. Their plight went unnoticed in the rest of Europe, which was understandably preoccupied with surviving World War II—a war which really began in Spain. General Franco went on to establish a dictatorship which lasted until 1975, when he died in bed of old age.

2

A QUICK GUIDE TO THE INTERNATIONAL BRIGADES IN 20 QUESTIONS AND ANSWERS

1. What were the International Brigades?

The men and women of the International Brigades were anti-fascist volunteers from outside Spain who wanted to fight for the Republic against the Nationalist uprising.

2. How many volunteers joined up?

Estimates of the total number of volunteers who went to Spain range from 35,000 to 45,000, although the exact number will never be known. Accurate records of volunteers coming in from all over the world have been lost, destroyed, or were never kept in the first place. Not all the volunteers were there at the same time—it is estimated that there were never more than 20,000 in the country simultaneously—as people came and went throughout the Civil War. And some volunteers, such as George Orwell, made their own way and not as part of the International Brigades' organization.

3. Where did the volunteers come from?

The volunteers came from fifty different countries. In the 1930s there were far fewer sovereign nations than today—many

A unit from the Bulgarian International Brigade under the command of Ivan Bitsov, 1937. (Wikimedia Commons)

countries have only established themselves with post-World War II decolonization—so this was a high percentage of the global total. The largest national group was from neighboring France. The French were followed by German and Italian exiles and volunteers from Poland, Central Europe, and the Balkan states who knew exactly what the fascist threat meant. There were some 2,500 British and Irish volunteers, about the same number of Americans, and around 1,500 Canadians.

4. WHEN DID THE INTERNATIONAL BRIGADES ARRIVE IN MADRID?

Some individual volunteers made their way over to Spain in the summer of 1936. The first group of officially organized International Brigade volunteers arrived in Barcelona in the middle of October 1936. As Franco's army marched on Madrid the International Brigades were drafted in to help defend the city. The XI Brigade arrived on 8 November, just as the Nationalists were making their first assault.

5. What about the British volunteers?

The first British volunteers were among those who arrived in the summer and autumn of 1936. Some mixed in with the mainly French-speaking XI Brigade, while others joined the mainly German-speaking XII Brigade. For a while neither group was aware of the other's existence! By Christmas 1936 hundreds more British volunteers arrived. There were then enough to form a complete British battalion within the newly formed XV International Brigade. The first 100 or so US volunteers left New York on Christmas Day 1936 and arrived in Spain early in 1937.

6. Brigade? Battalion? Stop, I'm confused! What do these terms mean?

A brigade is the largest of these units—up to 5,000 men. Brigades are split into battalions of between 300 and 800 men. Each battalion is split into companies of around 100 men. There were between 500 and 600 men in the British battalion.

7. How many International Brigades were there?

Eventually there were five in total. They were added to ten existing Spanish brigades. That is why they became called the XI International Brigade, XII International Brigade, and so on. The British, Irish, American Lincoln Battalion, and Canadian MacKenzie-Papineau Battalion (known as the Mac-Pap) volunteers fought with the XV International Brigade.

8. Where Were They Based?

The Brigades' headquarters was at a town called Albacete, on the plain of La Mancha, about 250 kilometers to the southeast of Madrid. The British Battalion was based in a small town called Madrigueras, close to Albacete.

9. Where Did These Volunteers Fight in Madrid?

Some individual volunteers from different European countries fought on the frontline of the defense of Madrid in November 1936. By January 1937 there were enough British volunteers to form an entire British battalion. This fought at the Battles of Jarama (February 1937) and Brunete (July 1937) just outside the city. The battalion also fought in Andalucia in the south of Spain and on the Aragon front in the north. The American Abraham Lincoln Battalion also fought at Jarama, Brunete, and on the Aragon front.

10. Why Did the Volunteers Go to Fight in Madrid?

According to the legend on the International Brigade memorial on the south bank of the River Thames in London, "They went because their open eyes could see no other way." In Britain, Conservative governments pursued a policy of appeasement in the 1930s, caving in to the demands of the fascist and Nazi dictators on continental Europe in the hope of preventing all-out war. In Washington, the Roosevelt administration did not want to become embroiled in another European war or alienate the generally pro-Franco Catholic vote, an essential part of the Democratic Party's electoral base in places like New York and Boston. Appeasement had its critics in Britain—there were divisions within both the left and right—but for the first few months of the war in Spain there was broad support for the government's policy of non-intervention. Then it became clear that the Non-Intervention Agreement (see Chapter 1) was being systematically broken. The Communist Party of Great Britain, which had always opposed appeasement, felt vindicated and at that point many others threw in their lot with them. Many volunteers were communists—but by no means all. Albert Charlesworth from Oldham, for example, went to fight in Spain aged 21. By his own admission he was "not a political animal" but used to hang around the local Labour Club for the social life. There he read newspapers and became "indignant" at Franco's attempt to usurp power. When asked in later life exactly why he felt moved to go, he replied candidly, "I don't rightly know." Like Charlesworth many were moved as much by instinct to "do something" about the threat of fascism as by doctrinaire ideology.

11. Who organized the International Brigades?

The Brigades were organized by the Comintern, the international communist network based in Moscow. Entry to Spain was organized through the central International Brigade office in Paris. One Josef Brotz, known as Tito, helped deal with the paperwork and money for the volunteers. Marshal Tito later became President of Yugoslavia. Most British volunteers had to pass through the Communist Party's King Street headquarters in London's Covent Garden.

12. So they were just Stalin's stooges?

Not quite. Support for the volunteers and for the Republic went far beyond the Communist Party or even the left. In his memoirs, Conservative Prime Minister Edward Heath described the conflict in Spain as one which "aroused in our generation passions every bit as fierce as those stirred up by the Vietnam war" in the 1960s. In 1937 Heath was a student at Oxford and President of the University's Conservative Association, and was elected by the Conservative students on an anti-appeasement platform, defeating an opponent who was "a known Franco supporter." That year Heath joined an all-party group from Oxford on a visit to Spain. The group met leading Republican politicians for a dinner. The conversation, which went on until 3AM, "made clear to me, more than anything else at that time, the turbulent future my generation faced." The future Tory leader went on to record that "when the survivors of the [International] Brigade returned to London I joined colleagues from across the political spectrum at Victoria station to welcome them home."

One anecdote from Madrid illustrates the political cross-dressing of the time. The story goes that an all-party group of British MPs sympathetic to the Republic went on a fact finding mission to Madrid. At one point they heard the drone of aeroplane engines and began to take cover fearing an air attack. It then became apparent from the markings and design that they were Soviet planes fighting for the Republic. "Its OK," said a Tory MP to the relief—and amusement—of the others, "they're ours!"

13. DID THE NATIONALISTS ALSO USE FOREIGN TROOPS DURING THE SIEGE OF MADRID?

Yes, and many more than the Republicans. General Franco claimed that he was fighting to preserve the true Spanish identity and it was hence ironic that he relied so heavily on foreign troops for the self-appointed mission. It has been estimated that foreign nationals made up just 2.2 percent of the 1.8 million people who fought for the Republic. By contrast, some 13.4 percent of the Nationalist troops were non-Spanish. Franco himself led the Army of Africa, which was mainly comprised of Muslim Moroccans. Mussolini sent materiel and around 80,000 Italian troops to fight for Spanish nationalism. Hitler sent valuable arms, expertise, and men who were organized into what was called the Condor Legion. In addition there were small groups of pro-fascist foreign nationals. For example, scores of devout Irish Catholics went to fight for Franco as did a handful of British fascists. (See *Franco's International Brigades: Adventurers, Fascists and Christian Crusaders in the Spanish Civil War* by Christopher Othen.)

14. What kind of people fought with the International Brigades?

In the first few months they were mainly well-heeled individuals able to find their own way to Spain. Then, in the autumn of 1936, the recruitment drive organized by the Communist

Thousands of Moroccans—good Muslims to a man—were recruited to join the Nationalist Christian "crusade." German transporters lent by Hitler airlifted the men from Morocco to Andalucia. (http://nopurifyingfire.commons.yale.edu)

Party began in earnest and many more working-class men volunteered. It is calculated that around 80 percent of the volunteers were working-class, employed in mining, industry, transport, or trades, and that some 60 percent were communists. A significant proportion was not, however, and some members of the British Battalion formed a Clement Attlee Company, named after the leader of the Labour Party. (Incidentally, a morale-raising visit by Attlee to the British volunteers was not entirely successful.) Spanish speakers were bemused when, at the close of his address to the gathered troops, the Labour leader bellowed, "No pasarán! And no pasaremos!" (they will not get past and we will not get past).

Most volunteers were from the cities, and their ages ranged from those in their teens to people in their sixties. A recent study of the US Lincoln Battalion suggests that most were young: 70 percent of the volunteers were in their twenties. And not all were men. The first British person to die fighting for the Republic in Spain was a woman, Felicia Browne, who was killed in August 1936. Many women joined the Medical Aid for Spain, which provided essential nursing and ambulance driving support for the volunteers, while some women also fought in the Brigades themselves.

15. Were Any of the Volunteers Famous?

Authors George Orwell and Laurie Lee, comic actor James Robertson Justice, and trade union leader Jack Jones are all high on the list. The black opera singer Paul Robeson visited Spain to sing in concerts for the troops, while writers Ernest Hemingway and Martha Gellhorn or movie star Errol Flynn toured the front to gather material or boost morale. But perhaps the best-known volunteer was Rick Blaine, the hard-bitten bar owner played by Humphrey Bogart in the film *Casablanca*. Over a quiet drink the town's police chief Louis lets Rick know that they have a file on him revealing that he "fought with the Republicans in Spain." With that one line the audience suddenly understands that Rick's apparently disinterested cynicism is really a sham. He is a good guy after all.

16. What were conditions like for the volunteers?

Pretty bad. Equipment, food, pay, and leave were poor. Some of the volunteers had fought in World War I or been trained in the services—but not many. Most had never handled a gun in their lives. The few weeks they spent at the Brigade base before being thrown into battle did little to prepare them for the experience—one volunteer recalled, "we never wasted ammunition in training because there wasn't any." Rudimentary aids like maps were lacking too: International Brigade General Pavol Lukács was reduced to planning his strategy on the outskirts of Madrid using a map ripped out of an aged Baedeker guide to the city. Yet the Brigades were always in the frontline and often ordered to do things which other Republican troops were reluctant to do—studies suggest that casualty rates among the International Brigades were well above those for Spanish units. Leave was almost impossible to obtain (despite initial promises) and the volunteers were left for long periods at the front. Food was monotonous and many found it hard to adjust to a diet based on sardines, chickpeas, olive oil, and rough red wine. For those who had had enough, getting out was highly problematic. Officially they did not exist. They had no travel documents and because of the Non-Intervention Agreement should never have been in Spain. When volunteers from the US arrived in France on their way to Spain, for example, their passports were stamped "Not Valid for Travel in Spain." It was also alleged at the highest level that the Brigades had been infiltrated by fascists and Nazis. In his diary the President of the Republic, Manuel Azaña, recorded that "the International Brigades have many Nazi spies within. Some have been discovered and shot." On the other side, volunteers also made frequent complaints about the iron discipline of the Communist Party, which ran the Brigades through Spanish apparatchiks and a myriad of shady "advisors." This discipline was enforced by a political network which operated within the Brigades.

17. HOW EFFECTIVE WERE THE INTERNATIONAL BRIGADES? DID THEY REALLY MAKE A DIFFERENCE?

Winston Churchill disparagingly called the volunteers "armed tourists" but they were far more than that. Militarily, the Brigades made a significant difference during fighting across the university campus in November 1936 and later at the Battle of Jarama in February 1937 (see Chapter 6). The historian Hugh Thomas argued that the really important impact of the volunteers in the besieged city, however, was that their presence boosted morale: "The example of the International Brigades fired the populace of the capital with the feeling that they were not alone." Spanish Republicans felt abandoned by liberal democracies such as Britain, France, and the US. The Non-Intervention Agreement confirmed the Spanish government's fear that other democracies had either failed to understand the nature of the threat or were too afraid to deal with the rising tide of totalitarianism. The sense of isolation was also fueled by a deeper Spanish mood that Spain, once the most powerful country in the world, had dwindled as an imperial power and become a European backwater about which their neighbors cared little. The arrival of the International Brigades brought a new focus on Spain—and new hope to those defending Madrid.

18. WHEN AND HOW DID THE INTERNATIONAL BRIGADES LEAVE SPAIN?

At the end of October 1938—before the war was officially over. By the autumn of 1938 the Republic was clearly heading for defeat. The Prime Minister tried but failed to negotiate a truce with Nationalists, which included all foreign combatants leaving Spain. To demonstrate goodwill, the Republic bade farewell to the International Brigades. On 29 October a final parade was organized for the remaining volunteers through the center of Barcelona before they boarded the ships waiting to take them to France. Government ministers, along with thousands of ordinary people, turned out to salute the men. The charismatic Spanish communist leader, Dolores Ibárruri, known to one and all as "La Pasionaria," made a fiery speech in which she told the volunteers

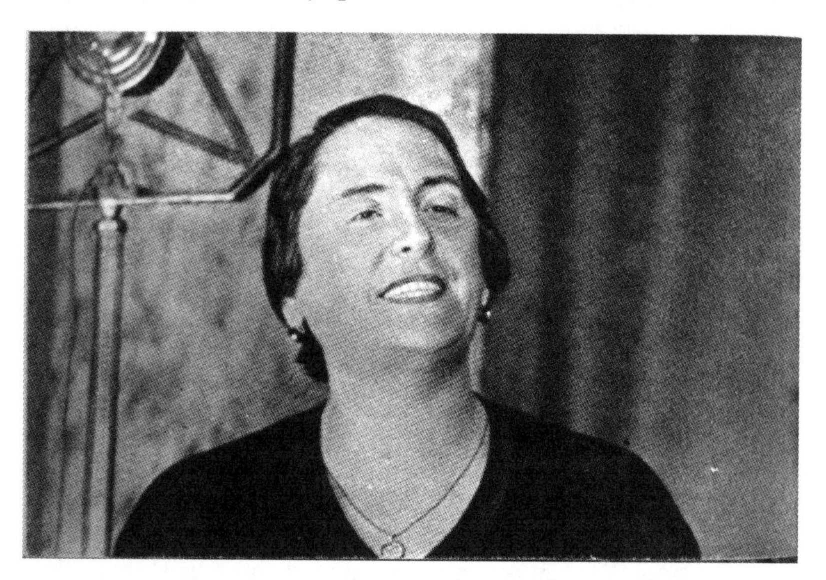

Dolores Ibárruri, "La Pasionaria," a communist deputy famed for her passionate speeches, in 1937. She told Madrileños that "it is better to die on your feet than live on your knees."
(Mikhail Koltsov/Wikimedia Commons)

they could leave with their heads held high: "you are legend, you are history." It was an emotional moment but a futile gesture by the Republic. Not surprisingly, Franco made no reciprocal offer to withdraw German or Italian troops and by then European fascism was well down the road to engaging in total war.

Thousands of the volunteers did not leave, of course. The casualty rates of the International Brigades were very high: it is estimated that between 9,000 and 10,000 volunteers died in Spain whilst many more were seriously wounded.

19. WHAT HAPPENED TO THE VOLUNTEERS AT THE END OF THE WAR?

By 1939 the nature of the fascist threat in Europe was clear to even the most myopic political observer. Franco's Nationalist army took control of Spain on 1 April 1939. A few months later Hitler invaded Poland and Britain declared war on Germany. A global conflict against the Axis powers was now inevitable. Having demonstrably been on the right side of history, many International Brigadiers now expected that they would be welcome in the wider fight against fascism. It was a reasonable assumption but completely wrong. Few of the Brigade veterans were incorporated as experienced, committed recruits in the war effort. Many were regarded as erratic radicals and refused admission into the armed services. Brigade veterans were frequently described as "premature anti-fascists"—an official euphemism for communist. On the day after Pearl Harbor, for example, all the surviving members of the Abraham Lincoln Battalion tried to enlist en masse into the US military. Their applications were refused, also en masse.

Nevertheless, some individuals managed to make important contributions. When one commander of the British battalion in Madrid, Tom Wintceringham, was refused entry into the British army he set up the Home Guard. We now associate this body with the antics of Captain Mainwaring and the popular television comedy *Dad's Army*, but Winteringham's initiative was very different. Had the Nazis invaded Britain they might have been met by the highly organized guerrilla warfare envisaged by Winteringham. Another battalion commander, Fred Copeman, was incapable of active service partly because of the wounds he sustained in Madrid. However, he was tasked with organizing air-raid shelters in Westminster. Part of the work included, ironically, making sure that members of the Royal Family were kept safe and sound. At the end of the war, with the British monarchy intact, he was awarded an OBE for his work. Copeman subsequently served for decades as a Labour councilor in the London borough of Lewisham, where there is now a street named after him—a rare memorial to an individual member of the International Brigades.

Members of an International Brigade disband, 1938.
(Wikimedia Commons)

20. Did any volunteers later regret their involvement in Spain?

Despite all the pitfalls and privations, the vast majority of volunteers remained immensely proud of the fight they put up. Alfred Sherman, for example, was a young communist who fought in Spain. Later in life his political views changed completely and he founded a free-market, rightwing think-tank which so influenced the policies of Margaret Thatcher that she gave him a knighthood. Yet Sherman continued to go to Brigade reunions until his dying day. Volunteer Jason Gurney explained why. In his short and movingly written memoir, Gurney makes no attempt to hide his disillusionment with the organization of the war: "There is no longer any point in trying to untangle the web of lies and confusion which lay behind the ghastly civil war. It arose out of total confusion and chaos." He was even more scathing about the role of the Communist Party and (like George Orwell) claimed that it treated the volunteers as "raw material" for the revolution. But Gurney then concludes that even in his moments of deepest depression after the war he "never regretted" his participation: "The manifest evils of fascism seemed as if it would overwhelm every value of Western civilization... The situation is not to be judged by what we now know of it but only as it appeared in the context of the period. And in that context there was a clear choice for anyone who professed to be opposed to fascism."

3

20 SPANISH CIVIL WAR SITES IN MADRID CITY CENTER: A QUICK GUIDE

1. Atocha Railway Station (Glorieta del Emperador Carlos V)

Sunday, 8 November 1936, was a gray, grim day. General Franco's troops had just begun their assault on Madrid (see Chapter Five). The city was fighting for its survival and most expected it to fall. Yet that morning some 2,500 members of the International Brigades arrived at the Atocha Railway Station to join the defense. After a long, interrupted journey from their base in Albacete, the volunteers were tired but taut with anticipation. They made their way down the platforms under the station's huge single-span steel arch designed by Alberto de Palacio—an associate of Gustave Eiffel—and mustered in the yard outside. Across the street was a giant billboard, with a somber message: "The Fascists murdered 2,000 people in Badajoz—Madrid will be next—we must defend ourselves."

Franco's forces were now just a couple of kilometers away. The Republic's government had fled the city for the safety of Valencia two days previously, followed by most of the international press corps. Just three British journalists had remained in the city to cover what they assumed would be another triumph for European fascism. The volunteers of the

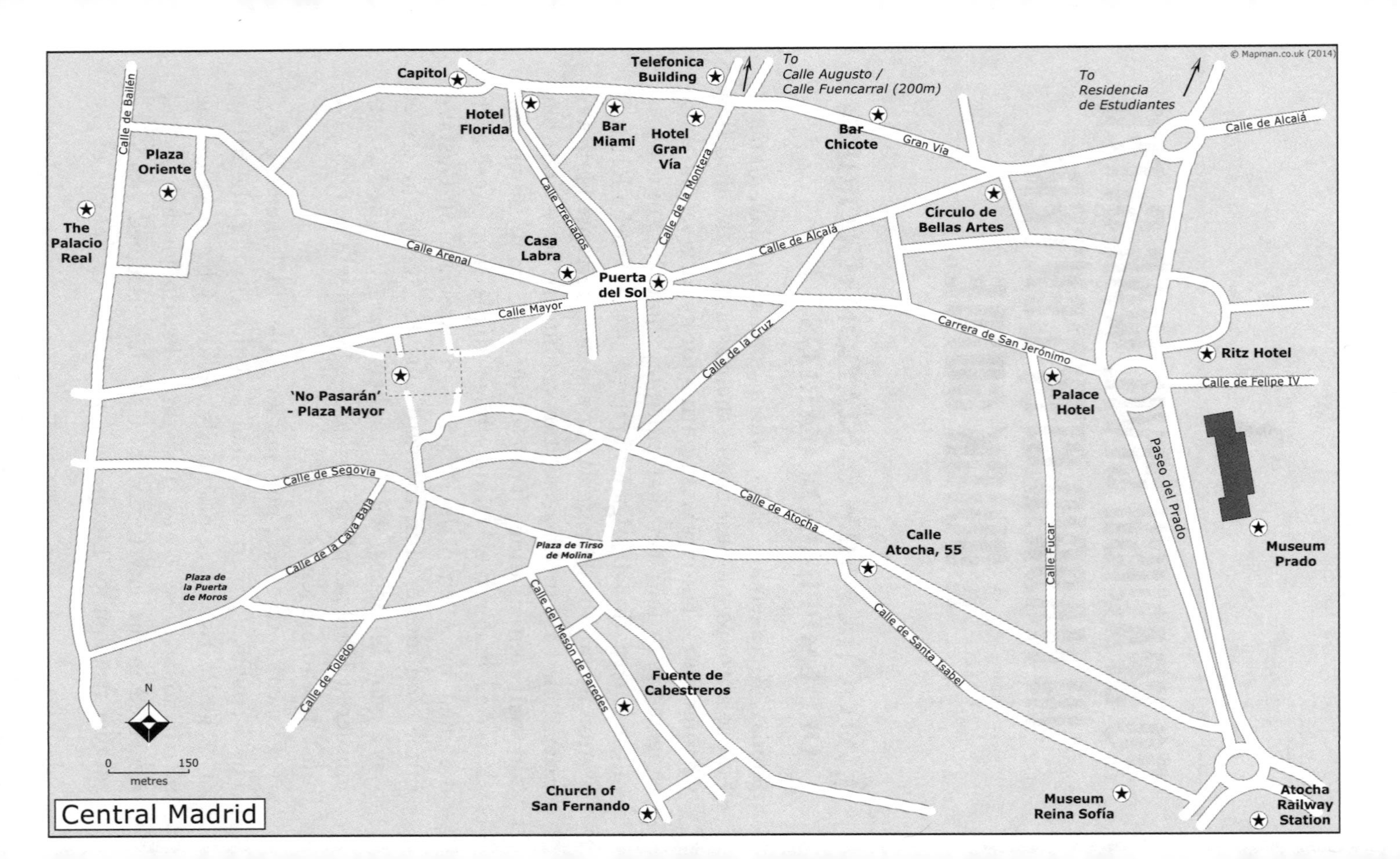

Central Madrid
© Mapman.co.uk (2014)
Capitol
Telefonica Building
To Calle Augusto / Calle Fuencarral (200m)
To Residencia de Estudiantes
Calle de Alcalá
Calle de Bailén
Plaza Oriente
The Palacio Real
Hotel Florida
Bar Miami
Hotel Gran Vía
Bar Chicote
Gran Vía
Calle Preciados
Calle de la Montera
Círculo de Bellas Artes
Calle Arenal
Casa Labra
Puerta del Sol
Calle de Alcalá
Calle Mayor
Carrera de San Jerónimo
Ritz Hotel
Calle de Felipe IV
Palace Hotel
'No Pasarán' - Plaza Mayor
Calle de la Cruz
Paseo del Prado
Calle de Segovia
Calle de Atocha
Museum Prado
Calle de la Cava Baja
Plaza de Tirso de Molina
Calle Atocha, 55
Calle Fucar
Plaza de la Puerta de Moros
Calle del Mesón de Paredes
Calle de Santa Isabel
Calle de Toledo
Fuente de Cabestreros
N
0
150
metres
Church of San Fernando
Museum Reina Sofía
Atocha Railway Station

International Brigades had different ideas, however, and began to march through deserted streets toward the front. It was a demonstration of courage which has entered into legend.

The Chilean poet Pablo Neruda evoked the scene: "one morning of a cold and dying month, stained with mud and smoke, I saw arriving those clear, dominating combatants with blue eyes... coming from far, far away." The Brigade, he said, was "silent and resolute, like bells before the dawn." Few had set foot in Madrid before. The march from Atocha that day was the most they ever saw of a city for which they were about to make the ultimate sacrifice.

The men moved off in formation up the Calle Atocha and then to the Puerta del Sol. They then marched up Calle Montera, swinging left at the top into Gran Vía and then onto the Plaza de España. At this point the three battalions went to different sectors of the front. One, which included the British volunteers, went directly up the street now called Princesa to the university campus. The second went down to the Casa de Campo, while the third battalion went to take up a position in the Parque del Oeste (see Chapter 5).

2. Museo Reina Sofía (Calle de Santa Isabel, 52)

The building opposite the Atocha station is today famous as the Reina Sofía art museum. There is an excellent collection of art from the Second Republic and the 1930s. The centerpiece of the collection is Pablo Picasso's most famous work, *Guernika.* This giant canvas depicts the horror of the Civil War in Spain but has universal appeal. It has been taken up around the globe as one of the iconic anti-war images of the twentieth century. The title came from the provincial Basque town of Guernika, which was razed during one afternoon in April 1937 by the German Luftwaffe. Hundreds of innocent civilians were killed in an attack which captured worldwide attention. The horrific innovation in aerial warfare—targeting a civilian population—appalled the international community and was a foretaste of what would happen to London and many other cities in the course of World War II. Picasso had, in fact, been working on ideas for a canvas to depict the suffering of the innocent in war well before the attack on Guernika—his first sketches were based on the aerial bombing of Madrid in November 1936. The Málaga-born artist was a staunch anti-fascist who had lived in Paris since the 1920s. This made him something of a wanted man when Nazi troops occupied Paris in 1940. When the Gestapo paid a visit to his studio, one officer picked up a postcard of the *Guernika* painting and demanded to know of Picasso, "did you do this?" "No," said Picasso "you did."

Picasso's huge canvass Guernika on display in the Reina Sofía museum. The painting was a protest against the Nationalist bombing of civilians in places like Madrid.
(Adam Jones Ph.D./Wikimedia Commons)

The connection between the Reina Sofía building and the Civil War pre-dates its current use as an art gallery. The building was constructed in the eighteenth century as a clinic. It was known as the San Carlos and it served as Madrid's general hospital. In 1936 the beds began to fill with wounded from the war, and after November injured soldiers began to arrive from the front. Many were from the International Brigades. By early November the building was overflowing with over 1,000 patients although there was worse to come.

By mid-November 1936 it became clear to the Nationalist commanders that Madrid was putting up a far more stubborn defense than had been expected and so a campaign of aerial bombing was stepped up. These raids had two objectives. The first was to destroy physical infrastructure in the city—General Franco said openly that he would prefer to "raze Madrid than leave it to the Marxists." Secondly, the rebels—and their German pilot allies—were also keen to find out what psychological effect bombing would have on the civilian population. San Carlos Hospital was high on their target list. During one raid the building had to be evacuated with more than 1,000 patients moved from their beds into the basement or other buildings. The French journalist Louis Delaprée saw how the "first bombs fell on the hospital... the old people who could move themselves scuttled from the wards and fell over each other as they went down the stairs. They huddled in the basement and fights broke out to get the safest places. Others too sick and infirm to move simply slid under the beds as best they could..." In fact, the raids seem to have stiffened civilian morale in Madrid, while people around the world were appalled by reports of the deliberate targeting of the sick and injured. Historian Antony Beevor argues that the raids on the San Carlos helped move international public opinion against Franco.

3. Museo Nacional del Prado (Paseo del Prado, 1)

The Prado Museum is one of the jewels of Madrid. Its walls are hung with precious works by Old Masters such as Velázquez, Goya, Titian, Tintoretto, and Bosch—to name but a few. When the Nationalists began shelling Madrid, the government became preoccupied with the safety of the irreplaceable works. President Manuel Azaña said that "the Prado Musuem is more important to Spain than either the monarchy or the Republic combined." He predicted that "in fifty years no one will remember me or General Franco but everyone will still know who Velázquez and Goya were..." Azaña even offered to shoot himself if the war destroyed any of the paintings.

Pablo Picasso was named as Director of the Prado and entrusted with the task of selecting the most valuable pieces for safe storage. Trucks arrived to spirit the priceless collection away from Madrid to Valencia although some efforts soon hit a snag. Various paintings were so large that they would not pass under a bridge on the Madrid-Valencia highway. The problem was only solved by digging down and lowering the level of the road under the bridge. Leading up from the Prado Museum is the Paseo de Recoletos. In 1937 this fine, tree-lined avenue was renamed Avenida de las Brigadas Internacionales in recognition of their contribution to the defense of Madrid. It was one of several street name changes which did not, of course, survive into the Franco dictatorship.

4. & 5. The Ritz Hotel (Plaza de la Lealtad, 5) and Palace Hotel (Plaza de las Cortes, 7)

Two of the swankiest hotels in Madrid were requisitioned for use as hospitals during the Civil War. Both were built following the coronation of King Alfonso XIII in 1905 when the new monarch was embarrassed to discover that Madrid lacked quality hotel space for his aristocratic guests who came from all over Europe to attend the ceremony. The Palace Hotel, opposite the Spanish parliament, opened in 1912. For the first few weeks of the war the fine Art Nouveau building was used to house the Soviet Embassy. Many important meetings were convened here by the ambassador, Marcel Rosenberg. During the late autumn and winter of 1936 the role of the Spanish Communist party, backed by Soviet "advisors" and weapons from the USSR, became increasingly important. Franco had welded together different factions on the right. As *caudillo,* or supreme leader, he assumed not just a unitary military command but total political control of the Nationalist side. For their part, the communists sought—with only partial success—to achieve something similar on the Republican side. Soviet dictates, however, frustrated Republican leaders, especially Prime Minister Largo Caballero. Ironically, Largo, who had once declared himself to be "the Spanish Lenin," now fumed about the Soviet ambassador ordering him around "like a Russian Viceroy in Spain." Then—a further irony—Stalin abruptly brought Largo's torment to an end. Rosenberg was recalled to Moscow in February 1937 and eliminated soon after in the purges. Largo had little time to capitalize on his freedom of action, though. He was heavily criticized for this conduct of the war and sacked as Prime Minister a few weeks later.

In the winter of 1936 the Palace was converted into a hospital and offices. Wounded soldiers from the frontline were treated there along with civilians injured in the bombing. Journalist Virgina Cowles described what she saw at the hotel at the time as "unforgettable... The steps were spattered with blood and the lobby was crowded with wounded men on stretchers waiting to be operated on."

The operating theater was set up on the ground floor in the hotel's famous rotunda where customers can now enjoy a heftily priced coffee or beer.

Over the road, Madrid's Ritz Hotel was opened in 1910. During the conflict the ground floor became a people's food kitchen. Bedrooms were turned over to use by medical personnel tending to the injured. Ironically it was here—in possibly Madrid's plushest hotel—that the legendary anarchist leader Buenaventura Durruti died in Room 27 on the first floor on 20 November 1936. Durruti had been mortally wounded while observing the vicious fighting around the Hospital Clínico the previous day (see Chapter 5). The fatal injury was caused by a single bullet, though where the shot came from remains a mystery. A Nationalist sniper, an accident (some accounts say that Durruti's own gun caught his car door handle), or a disgruntled volunteer from the Durruti Column (an anarchist military unit) have all been identified as the killer. Bleeding profusely, the anarchist leader was taken to a makeshift operating theater in the Ritz. Doctors pronounced that the wound was fatal. An eminent surgeon operating on the wounded in the Palace Hotel across the road arrived to offer a second opinion. He agreed that nothing could be done. Durruti was dosed up with morphine, entered into a coma at around midnight, and died between 4 and 5AM.

Coincidentally, at this same hour the Falangist leader José Antonio Primo de Rivera was preparing to walk out of his prison cell in Alicante and face a firing squad. The two men, on opposite ends of the Spanish political spectrum which led to the Civil War, died within hours of each other and became iconic figures for their followers. When Durruti's body was taken for burial in Barcelona hundreds of thousands of people followed the cortege in one of the biggest street demonstrations ever seen in Spain. And then his legend lived on into the vibrant Manchester music scene in the 1980s. One of the best post-punk rock bands to come out of the city called itself the Durutti Column—a homage to the man if not an accurate spelling of his name.

6. Círculo de Bellas Artes (Calle de Alcalá, 42)

During the Civil War this handsome art center in central Madrid was effectively a factory of Republican propaganda and home to a group called Altavoz del Frente (Loudspeaker of the Front). Artists worked tirelessly on cinema, theater, and visual art to support the war effort. The workshops churned out giant hoardings which were erected around the city. Slogans proclaimed that "Madrid will be the Tomb of Fascism" and repeated that the Nationalists would not enter (*No Pasarán*). Some of this art work is now on display in the Reina Sofia gallery along with Picasso's *Guernika.* Competitions were organized encouraging ordinary people to contribute their artwork or writing. One was to provide the words for a "Hymn for the Defence of Madrid." This was presumably more succesful than subsequent attempts to put words to the Spanish national anthem. Even in the democratic, post-Franco Spain the deep divisions which were a cause and consequence of the Civil War remain. The Spanish national anthem is still today without words because there is no national consensus about what they should be.

The Bellas Artes building has, however, a more sinister history than that of paints and paper. It was one of the *checas* where opponents of the Republic were detained and tortured by Communist Party militia. The original Russian *tcheka* network was founded to root out counter-revolutionary saboteurs after the 1917 Revolution: the founder Felix Dyerjinsky said that "the tcheka do not understand clemency and are implacable." This organization then developed into the feared NKVD and KGB, Stalin's secret police. The *checas* in Madrid were set up for a similar purpose. In the summer of 1936 security in the capital was chaotic. Political militias from different political groupings also set about hunting down opponents who might sabotage the war effort. While government ministers called for calm, the hunt for the fifth columnists spiraled out of control. Suspects were taken for a *paseo* or walk in the Parque del Oeste or Casa de Campo where they were summarily assassinated. Some genuine threats to the Republic, like Falangist leader José Antonio Primo de Rivera, were locked up with justification. But even well-known bullfighters, actors, and soccer players, who had little if anything to do with the rebellion, were caught up in the mayhem. Order was only really restored as the Nationalist army approached the city. The militia were then merged into a more disciplined force focused on defending Madrid from imminent threat.

The Círculo de Bellas Artes is now home to art studios, a theater, cinema, and bars. It is a good place to stop off for a coffee and the view over Madrid from the roof terrace is spectacular.

7. Calle Atocha, 55

On 27 January 1977 a group of labor lawyers were chatting in their office. It was late in the evening and the day's work was over but none wanted to leave just yet. These were heady days. General Franco had been dead for little over a year. Spain was in the turmoil of the transition from dictatorship to the possible dawn of a new democratic age. For these lawyers and their friends—sympathizers all of the still banned Communist Party—there was a lot to talk about. Their office was a meeting point for clandestine supporters of the left and nobody was surprised when the door bell rang at around 10:30. The visitors, however, were not comrades come to talk strategy or swap gossip. They were a Falangist hit squad. When the gunmen opened fire in the small office five people were killed instantly and the other four seriously wounded. The killers then walked coolly out into Calle Atocha and the bustle of central Madrid. The assassins clearly expected popular support and official approval for their action. Killing communists had, after all, been part of the Spanish national make-up for more than four decades by this time. But the Falangists badly misjudged the new mood and the murders revolted a broad range of Spanish society. Hardly anyone wanted a return to the bitterness, political assassinations, and deadly *pasesos* associated with the Civil War. The Abogados de Atocha (Atocha lawyers) became martyred folk heroes of the transition and a rallying point for all those determined to build a new Spain. The statue of the huddled group which now stands outside their office represents more than just grief. It is an eloquent cry for unity in a city which all too often has been scarred by division.

8. Puerta del Sol

A cold cup of coffee stood on the bar of a café in the Puerta del Sol for much of the war. It had been placed there by the owner, mocking the Nationalist General Mola's boast that he would be taking coffee in the Puerta del Sol by the middle of October 1936. The coffee went unclaimed. Mola, who was killed in a plane crash in the summer of 1937, never did make it to Madrid.

Sol, as it is popularly known, has been the geographical, cultural, and political center of Madrid life for centuries. The square is dominated by the building which is now municipal offices. It was here that an ecstatic crowd greeted the proclamation of the the Second Republic on 14 April 1931 (the announcement was made from the balcony beneath the clock tower). On 18 July 1936 the crowds returned again, this time in a more somber mood. They demanded that the government release weapons so that the militia groups could defend the city against the rebels (this is the subject of Chapter 4). Immediately behind the Town Hall is the Plaza de Pontejos and the police station where José del Castillo was based. It was his murder which was the immediate trigger for war (see Chapter 1).

On 18 November 1936 a colossal bomb landed on the entrance to the Metro station at the junction between the Puerta del Sol and the Calle de Alcalá. It blew a crater 15 meters deep, exposing the rails of the Metro track beneath. The French journalist Louis

Crater left by the explosion of a massive bomb dropped on the Puerta del Sol in the center of Madrid. (Ministerio de Educación, Cultura y Deporte, Archivo General de la Administración [Archivo Rojo])

Delaprée described the raid: "Then the great massacre began. The horror of the apocalypse. The murderers moved around freely in the air dropping explosive bombs, incendiary bombs, and torpedoes." From the Blitz to nuclear bombs and drone strikes, we are now familiar with the targeting of civilian populations from the air. In 1936, however, this type of warfare was still in the experimental stage. If Madrid was the laboratory, Sol was one of the test tubes for the new *blitzkrieg* strategy.

9. Casa Labra (Calle Tetuán 12)

On 2 May 1879, five doctors, two jewelers, a stonemason, a carpenter, and sixteen printers met up in a bar to talk. Nothing new there perhaps, but this gathering changed the history of Spain. The group wanted to launch a political party and met clandestinely because political meetings were illegal at the time. Nevertheless they pushed on and pledged to found the Partido Socialista Obrero Español or Spanish Socialist Workers' Party (PSOE). The decision taken in the Casa Labra makes the PSOE Europe's second oldest socialist party, after the German SPD. Despite the illegitimate birth, the PSOE became the largest party on the Spanish left and a reference point for the country's politics in the twentieth century. PSOE politicians played key roles during the Second Republic and Civil War—some effectively, some not, while many of the party's members engaged in the fighting. The leadership was forced into exile during Franco's dictatorship but came back to dominate Spanish politics after his death. Today the historic Casa Labra bar is a great place to stop off for a drink and snack.

10. Corner of Calle Fuencarral with Calle Augusto Figueroa

José del Castillo was a young officer of the Assault Guards, an official Republican security force. On the sultry evening of 12 July 1936 Castillo walked from his home to work down the

Calle Fuencarral. He had been married for just a few weeks and had spent the afternoon at the bullring with friends watching the fights. Despite the turbulence in the city, life was good. As he crossed the Calle Augusto Figueroa, the young officer was felled by a hail of bullets from a rightwing hit squad. Like the shots which killed the Archduke Franz Ferdinand in Sarejevo in 1914, this assassination triggered a chain of events which led to bloody conflict. Castillo's *compañeros* murdered a leading rightwing politician in revenge the following night. Events generated their own momentum. On 17 July the military uprising began and Spain was at war with itself.

11. Edificio Telefónica (Telefonica Building) (Calle Gran Vía, 28)

At around midday on 8 November 1936 the newly arrived column of the XI International Brigade volunteers came to a halt halfway down the Gran Vía. Outside one of Madrid's most prestigious landmarks, the Telefónica Builiding, they basked in the cheers and applause of *Madrileños.* It was a moment which has entered into the International Brigades' folklore.

The Telefónica tower was one of the tallest buildings in Europe when it was opened in 1930. King Alfonso XIII exclaimed with pride at the inauguration that "no one can now say that Africa begins at the Pyrenees" (an age-old jibe about Spain's underdevelopment). The building was owned by the US International Telephone and Telegraph Company and was a communications hub. The American writer and journalist John Dos Passos regularly filed stories from the building during the war. He mused that it "seemed funny that the least Spanish building in Madrid, the tower which was a symbol of the colonizing Dollar, should have become in the mind of Madrileños a symbol of the defense of the city." The building

The Telefónica Building in the center of Madrid was intended to symbolize the modernization of Spain when it opened in 1930. It was extensively shelled by Nationalist artillery batteries throughout the war. (Catriona Davidson)

was a hive of activity during the conflict. The top floors of the 14-story structure, which had spectacular views of the frontline to the north and west, were used as an observation platform by Republican military commanders and their Soviet advisors, such as Colonel Nikolai Voronov. He went on to command the Soviet artillery at Stalingrad—and took the Nazi General Paulus' surrender there when the Germans were defeated.

The lower floors continued to function as a communications center and telephone exchange despite the battle raging literally down the street. The fourth floor was the international press center where journalists of all nationalities crowded together in smoke-filled offices to prepare their stories. Once finalized for transmission, all copy had to be approved by one of the Republic's censors who worked on the floor above. There were only two phones for the entire press corps. When a journalist filed copy, reading it out slowly over the crackling line, the censor sat opposite. Deviation of just one word from the agreed text was enough to have the censor's hand slam down on the receiver and cut the line.

In the two-story basement there was enough room for around 1,300 people to shelter when the city was being shelled. And shelled it was, on an almost daily basis. While the Telefónica Building was an excellent center from which Republican commanders could observe the frontline, it was also a gift for Nationalists. The rebel artillery was positioned on the Cerro Garabitas (Garabitas Hill) in the Casa de Campo. The tall, white Telefónica Building, which dominated the center of the city, was a perfect range finder for the Nationalist gunners, a target in itself and also used to seek out other targets around the city. Gran Vía became known as "Death Avenue." Rebel artillery attacks were frequently timed to coincide with the end of the films at the many cinemas along Gran Vía—when they knew that the street would be thronged with people.

12. Bar Chicote (Calle Gran Vía, 12)

This legendary bar was a favorite hang-out during the war for soldiers and members of the International Brigades—"the good guys" as Ernest Hemingway described them. Hemingway himself was a regular and used the bar as a backdrop for his work. Chicote is the setting for a scene of the only play which he ever wrote about the war, *The Fifth Column,* and it features in several of his short stories. In the *Butterfly and the Tank,* Hemingway describes returning to his hotel after filing some copy on a wet December evening. "It was the second winter of shelling in the siege of Madrid and everything was short including tobacco and people's tempers and you were a little hungry all the time." Unable to resist the lure of Chicote's doorway, Hemingway decides to "get a quick one and then do those six blocks up the Gran Via through the mud and rubble of the streets broken by the bombardment." Despite the war Chicote was in full swing. "The place was crowded. You couldn't get near the bar and all the tables were full. It was full of smoke, singing, men in uniform, and the smell of wet leather coats, and they were handing out drinks over a crowd that was three deep at the bar."

The eponymous bar was an instant success from the moment it was opened in 1931 by Perico Chicote, the former head barman of the Palace Hotel. Cocktails were the speciality then, as they are now. The interior has been substantially revamped since 1930s, and the name changed to Museo Chicote, but the bar is still packed in the evening.

13. Hotel Gran Vía (Calle Gran Vía, 25)

Opposite the Telefónica Building, this hotel was the convenient haunt of the many journalists in Madrid to cover the war. Geoffrey Cox of the *News Chronicle,* Henry Buckley of the *Daily Telegraph,* and Sefton Delmer of the *Daily Mail* were among the British press pack who stayed here. Winston Churchill's nephew,

Esmond Romilly, was an early International Brigade volunteer and visited the hotel while on leave. Delmer had interviewed Romilly on a visit to the front just days earlier and met him by chance in the street. The journalist took pity on Romilly's grubby appearance and invited the soldier back for a bath—the hotel was one of the few which still had hot running water. Another guest was the Canadian medic, Dr. Norman Bethune, who pioneered the use of a field blood transfusion service. Bethune developed techniques to store blood taken from civilians which could then be transported and infused into soldiers wounded in the Casa de Campo. The innovation saved countless lives in Spain and was later used in World War II.

The government-run restaurant in the basement of the Hotel Gran Vía was reputed to serve the best food of any during the war—although there was little competition as many restaurants closed and conditions deteriorated as the siege went on. Even at the Gran Vía the menu was basic. Diners were served whatever could be foraged: vegetables, chickpeas cooked in olive oil, and bacalao (salted cod) or pickled sardines washed down with copious amounts of red wine. There might be an orange for dessert. Not surprisingly, most foreigners brought as much food as they could carry with them and certainly ate better than the *Madrileños.* The Nationalist blockade had also cut the supply of coal from the mines of Asturias in the north of the country so as winter drew on there was little in the way of heating even in the best hotels. Dinner was taken early—certainly by Madrid standards—at 7 or 8PM. Locals and visitors alike then tried to keep warm by going to bed by 9PM. One journalist slept in her clothes in an only partially successful attempt to keep warm during the chilly nights while another complained that her fingers stuck to the keys of her typewriter with cold.

Getting around was difficult. Many buses and most of the city's 3,000 or so taxis were requisitioned, along with their drivers, into the war effort. In any event there was little reason to go out as Madrid's famous nightlife was abruptly halted by the onset of the siege in November 1936. Conditions relaxed gradually but constant shelling made the center of Madrid a hazardous place to go for a drink.

14. Bar Miami (Calle Gran Via, 31)

The Bar Miami was a pre-war favorite of Madrid's smart set. During the siege of Madrid it became very popular with off-duty military and, conveniently opposite the Telefónica Building, it was also handy for thirsty journalists. The bar closed down in 2010 and is now a clothes store.

News Chronicle reporter Geoffrey Cox described the grubby, crowded, smoky bar with its classic, if slightly dated, jazz selection as one of the "in" places to go. The bar was dominated by a huge painting of men and women reclining languidly on a beach under the summer sun—a scene which sat incongruously alongside the clientele of war-torn Madrid. John Cornford was one of those who enjoyed a night in the Miami. Following his head wound fighting at the university, Cornford was given leave. He and his friends headed for the Miami and even when the Gran Vía came under yet another Nationalist artillery barrage, Cornford refused to budge from the bar. Apart from finishing his drink, the young British volunteer wanted to demonstrate the determination of the International Brigades who had come to the city. It was, in fact, one of his last nights out. Cornford was redeployed to the Andalucia front where he was killed on 28 December.

Geoffrey Cox described meeting up with Louis Delaprée on the evening of 7 December 1936 for a final drink. Dressed in a raincoat, red scarf, and gray felt hat, the dashing 34-year-old French journalist was drowning his sorrows. Delaprée was generally regarded as one of the finest journalists of his time and his reports of the defense of Madrid were among the very best. He had a litany of complaints though, the like of which have been expressed by foreign correspondents throughout the history of journalism. Life in Madrid, he declared, had become impossible and he was leaving the city. He was treated with suspicion in Madrid because everyone thought that his paper, *Paris Soir,* was pro-fascist. Meanwhile, the news desk in Paris spiked his stories because they thought them too pro-communist. And in any event, the readers seemed more interested in the year's ongoing scandal between Edward VIII and Mrs. Simpson than in reading about the hundreds of children being killed in Madrid. Delaprée left the bar for the last time that evening and walked out into the cold night air of the Gran Vía. The following day he boarded a French Embassy flight to Toulouse but never arrived. The plane was attacked soon after take off and crash landed in a remote field. It took more than a day to get Delaprée to a hospital, but by that time it was too late and he died soon afterwards. In one of his last pieces, Delaprée had expressed his frustration at the failure of European democracies to help the Republic. It had ended with the prophetic words, "God grant that all this blood in Spain will not choke you."

15. Hotel Florida (Plaza de Callao)

Guns, lies, and spies were the order of the day at the Hotel Florida during the Civil War. The clientele was a cosmopolitan crowd drawn to fight in, write about, or make money from the conflict. Off-duty soldiers, dodgy arms dealers, Russian advisors, journalists, prostitutes, and agents of all kinds were among the opaque characters with elliptical CVs who gave the hotel a unique ambience. Ernest Hemingway, a frequent guest, said that you could "learn as much at the Hotel Florida as you could learn anywhere in the world" during that time.

The building was less than a kilometer from the frontline. Guests had some excellent vantage points from which to view the action but the building was one of those most exposed to the fighting. Damage was inevitable, but through it all the

The Hotel Florida was a center of intrigue during the war.
(Wikimedia Commons)

hotel kept going. One journalist recalled that the chambermaid managed to keep her floor spotless, even if the end of the corridor had been blown away, giving a panoramic view over half of Madrid.

An International Brigade volunteer described the Florida as "a noisy bordello," while another said that the revelry and flamenco dancing were guaranteed to go well into the early hours every night. When *Daily Telegraph* correspondent Cedric Salter had trouble sleeping in his room because of a noisy party, he called down to complain. The night porter explained that some Russian pilots were "having fun" in the bar and that "it always went on like that until dawn unless they drank more than usual" (in which case they might fall asleep on the floor around 4AM). Salter had just managed to drop off himself when a naked woman came crashing into his room followed by a drunken Russian dressed only in his underpants. It took Salter some time to coax the pair back outside. On another night, an especially heavy Nationalist artillery bombardment forced guests to leave their rooms and the resulting scene was like a surreal, literary soirée. Authors Ernest Hemingway, Martha Gelhorn, John Dos Passos, and Claud Cockburn, all in Madrid to cover the war as journalists, emerged from their rooms in pajamas and dressing gowns. They shuffled along the corridors along with the usual exotic habitués and so many half-dressed prostitutes that one observer described it as being like a lingerie parade.

Sadly the hotel, which stood on the corner of Gran Vía and Plaza Callao, was demolished in 1964. The ubiquitous department store El Corte Inglés now stands on the site of the hotel, although much of the rest of the plaza remains as it was then.

16. Capitol (Calle Gran Vía, 41)

This building comprises both a hotel and the largest cinema in Madrid. One of the most modern buildings along the Gran Vía (it was completed in 1933), the complex was designed in the rationalist style. Three years later it was just a kilometer from the front line of Madrid and the madness of the Civil War. The Capitol played an important role in the war for a couple of reasons. The hotel was uncomfortably close to the fighting and attracted few guests. The top floors were then given over to lookouts who could observe fighting along the front from the roof of the Capitol. The cinema was also an important center for political meetings and screening films. Some movies were political propaganda: the President of the Republic and senior ministers were all in attendance when the Department of Cultural Propaganda organized a showing of the Eisenstein classic *Battleship Potemkin* about the Russian Revolution. The façade of the cinema was covered with an enormous poster and the interior bedecked with the banners of the communist 5th Regiment. Other films, though, were exercises in simple escapism to help people try and forget the horror of war. Charlie Chaplin, Laurel and Hardy, Joan Crawford, and Clark Gable were among the screen stars who tried to bring some light relief to the *Madrileños*. This was a difficult task as the Gran Vía was frequently shelled, especially at times when audiences were leaving. Whatever the film, the communist anthem *The Internationale* was always played and the audience would rise as one to sing the revolutionary chorus—except on one occasion when a militiaman remained firmly in his seat. Others turned on the man and began to hurl insults. "Why should I stand up?" cried the man angrily. "I am as patriotic as any of you but I've been at the front all day and I'm tired."

17. Church of San Fernando and the Fuente de Cabestreros, Lavapiés (Calle del Mesón de las Paredes)

19 July 1936 was one of the most turbulent days in Spanish history. News of the *coup d'état* declared by Franco and the other generals the previous day had now reached Madrid. Violence flared across the capital as forces loyal to the Republic clashed with others supporting the rebels. At the Church of San Fernando, in the historic working-class quarter of Lavapíes, a group of Falangists were engaged in a pitched battle with anarchist militiamen. Holed up inside the church, the Falangists mounted a machine gun on the cupola and initially resisted attempts to flush them out. Yet within hours they were dead and the building was a looted, blazing ruin. It stayed that way for the next four decades, the charred walls and broken dome a somber reminder of the uprising. The site was declared one of National Cultural Interest in 1996. Apart from the tragic events of 1936, San Fernando was of interest as one of Madrid's oldest churches. The impressive cupola dates back to the 1760s and the school attached to the

church was the first in Spain to admit deaf and dumb pupils. In 2002 the interior was imaginatively restored and converted into a library. It is now open to the viewing public at the end of every working day.

About 200 meters up the Calle del Mesón de las Paredes, on the corner with Calle Cabestreros, is a drinking fountain and tap. The clear inscription reads: República Española - 1934. This is odd as most public inscriptions referring to the Republic were erased under the Francoist dictatorship. How this survived is a mystery; perhaps the back streets of a working-class quarter like Lavapiés were of little interest to anyone in the regime. Nevertheless, the fountain remains an interesting piece of social history which transformed the lives of many in its time. Bringing an accessible supply of fresh water to working-class districts was one of the real social improvements made by the Second Republic. Such reforms had their critics on the Nationalist side, however, among them Franco's press spokesman, Gonzalo Aguilera. In 1937 Aguilera stunned foreign journalists when he told them that "modern sewer systems caused this war because unimpeded natural selection would have killed off most of the 'red' vermin." He cited the President of the Republic, Manuel Azaña, as a "typical case... He might have been carried off by infant paralysis but he was saved from it by these cursed sewers. We've got to do away with sewers." Aguilera went on to explain that "there are two races in Spain—a slave race and a ruler race." Other reforms, like the Republic's drive to promote universal education, were scornfully dismissed too. "It is sufficient for the masses to know just enough reading to understand orders. We must restore the authority of the Church." Opinions like these, and the Cabestreros fountain, go some way to explaining why the people of Lavapiés and similar districts remained fiercely loyal to the Republican government throughout the war.

18. Residencia de Estudiantes (Calle Pinar, 21-23, behind Museo Nacional de Ciencias Naturales)

To see this building as merely and literally a students' hall of residence would be rather to miss the point, rather like describing 10 Downing Street as just another terraced house. The Residencia is an oasis in the intellectual history of Spain and has been designated as a Centre of European Culture. Three of the student residents who were there together in the 1920s were Federico García Lorca, Salvador Dalí, and Luis Buñuel. Other guests before the war included Albert Einstein, John Maynard Keynes, Marie Curie, Igor Stravinsky, Walter Gropius, Henry Bergson, and Le Corbusier.

In the corridor outside Room 135 in the building called Gemelo II is a plaque made of glazed Spanish tiles (the center's friendly staff will point the way). The simple inscription reads "to the memory of the British writers who offered their lives in the name of Spanish democracy - John Cornford, Christopher Caldwell, Charles Donnelly, Ralph Fox, and Julian Bell." It is fitting that the memorial should be in the Residencia, which was opened in 1910 as the first liberal cultural center in Spain. One bedroom, preserved as it was and open to public view, is decorated with original furnishings from the 1920s. It looks like a Bloomsbury apartment of the era, self-consciously English. There is also an exhibition area which explains more about the history of the Residencia and the people who have stayed there.

Apart from the plaque to the British writers there are important historical connections between the Residencia and the Civil War. On the outbreak of war the Director was forced into exile and given refuge in Oxford. Others were less fortunate. In the first days of the conflict García Lorca, who had lived here, fled Madrid and sought refuge in his native Granada. It did not save him. He was hunted down and assassinated by a Falangist hit squad. Another frequent visitor was the philosopher and Rector of Salamanca University, Miguel Unamuno. On 12 October 1936 he made some of the most famous comments of the Civil War—words which ultimately cost him his life. 12 October is the Spanish national day and that year was celebrated with a patriotic ceremony in the Great Hall of Salamanca. The event was highly charged. Salamanca was a hotbed of Castilian nationalism and Franco's HQ was just a few hundred meters from the university. Speaker after speaker vilified the "red" Republic in the most inflammatory terms. The temperature rose further when one speaker described the Basques and Catalans as a "cancer on the body of Spain." Franco, he said, would be the unsentimental surgeon prepared to use the scalpel as the situation demanded. At this, a large contingent of Falangists leapt to their feet with right arms outstretched in the fascist salute. They were whipped to a frenzy by their *de facto* leader, General Millán Astray. The one-armed, one-eyed, battle-mutilated founder of the Spanish Foreign Legion was lionized by the Spanish right. He and his supporters launched into chants including "Spain—Great! United! Victorious!" "Long live death" and "Death to intellectuals."

The elderly Unamuno had not intended to say anything during the ceremony but now rose from his Rector's chair. An early supporter of the military revolt, he had privately come to regret his backing for the generals and what he had just witnessed confirmed his worst fears. A tense silence gripped the Great Hall of the ancient university. Clutching a few hastily scribbled notes, the old man quietly tore into Millán Astray and the ideology of the radical right. "There are times," he told them, "when to remain silent is to lie. I am unable to remain silent. Just now we heard the senseless and necrophiliac cry: 'long live death.' As a philosopher I have spent my life trying to resolve paradoxes... but let me tell you that this paradox is repellent to me. This is a temple of the intellect. You profane its sacred precincts." Unamuno observed that Millán Astray was "a cripple, a war invalid" though not, he insisted, to denigrate the general—he reminded his audience that the great Spanish writer Cervantes had also been mutilated by war. "But"—and here came the sting—"it pains me to think that this General will now dictate the pattern of mass psychology. A cripple who lacks the greatness of Cervantes may seek ominous relief in causing mutilation all around him... Unfortunately, there are too many cripples in Spain just now. And soon there will be more of them."

By now the silence was broken by angry shouts from around the Hall, but Unamuno ploughed on. "You will win because you have more than enough brute force. But you will not convince. Because to convince you need to persuade. And in order to persuade you would need what you lack: reason and right." A spitting mob of armed Falangists surrounded the Rector and many observers thought that he was about to be killed where he stood. Only the intervention of Franco's wife, Carmen Polo, who was on the platform, saved the old man. She slipped her arm into Unamuno's and escorted him from the Hall.

Polo's intervention spared Franco from an embarrassing incident—the murder of one of Spain's most high profile public intellectuals. But the revenge of the regime was swift and the old man's career finished. He was immediately dismissed from the university and socially ostracized. From then on Unamuno walked in fear for his life. Two months later, on 31 December 1936, he died a broken man. Unamuno personified the progressive, liberal, and rational forces which struggled courageously with the dilemmas of 1930s Spain. His phrase that night in Salamanca, *venceréis pero no convenceréis* (you will win but you will not convince), has become one of the most famous taunts against thuggery in the Spanish language. That spirit of rational thought is enshrined in the Residencia.

Today the Residencia continues to host students and organize a varied program of events. The café/bar is open to non-residents and is a welcoming place to stop for a drink and a snack.

19. The Palacio Real, Plaza de Oriente

There is an excellent view of the mountains of the Sierra de Guadarrama from the Plaza de Oriente in front of the Royal Palace. In the early weeks of the war, the President of the Second Republic Manuel Azaña was moved to tears as he stood in the palace looking out at the view and listening to the sound of gunfire. "So many Spaniards killing each other," he lamented. Later General Franco addressed huge crowds from the main balcony. They were not especially memorable rallies. Franco well knew that he was a poor public speaker and did not enjoy the occasions.

20. *No Pasarán* banner, Plaza Mayor

This slogan, meaning "they will not pass" or "they will not get through" in English, was on a banner slung above the Calle de Toledo where it enters the Plaza Mayor in the heart of the city. It is one of the most enduring images of the siege of Madrid and the slogan has been used by anti-fascists ever since.

Getting Around

Any of the places listed above can be visited as separate sites. They are all in the center of Madrid and easily accessible on foot or by bicycle. The only exception is the Residencia de Estudiantes (18), which is some 30 minutes walking distance from the Círculo de Bellas Artes (6).

Bike rental is available in the center of Madrid. The following outlets have rental bikes available by the hour or day. Riber Bike is at 12 Plaza de España (next to Templo Debod in Parque del Oeste—basic English spoken). See www.riberbike.es. Urbanmovil.com is a bike shop in 18 Calle Santiago (between the Royal Palace and Plaza Mayor—basic English spoken). In addition, Madrid has a system of self-hire electric bikes run by the town hall. These can be picked up at any number of on-street bike points around the city and dropped off at other points. Payment by credit card at €3 per hour.

¡No Pasarán!: this legendary slogan came to symbolize the resistance of Madrid during the siege. (Mikhail Koltsov/Wikimedia Commons)

4

THE MASSACRE AT THE MONTAÑA BARRACKS

"We rushed the Montaña barracks
With some old pistols and our bare hands
through the swiveling machine gun fire.
I was there.
I saw the officers cowering,
Their faces chalked with fear."
Jack Lindsay, 1937

After the heat and dust of a busy day in Madrid, there are few more pleasant places to be in the evening than what is known locally as the Parque Debod, the southernmost part of the extensive Parque del Oeste. Tourists and locals alike hang out amongst the trees and listen to busking musicians while the sun sets over the distant mountains of the Sierra de Guadarrama. It is now a cool place to be in every sense of the word, but this park also has a hidden, darker past and was a critical flashpoint of the Civil War.

In the summer of 1936 this was the site of an army base known as the Cuartel de la Montaña (Montaña Barracks). When the uprising was declared on 18 July, the soldiers in the Montaña had to decide whether to support the *coup* attempt or remain loyal to the Republic. It was literally a life or death decision. If they joined the uprising and it failed, the punishment for disloyalty to the Republic would be severe. On the other hand, if they remained loyal to the Republic and the uprising succeeded, they could expect no clemency from the generals.

Their decision would also be crucial for the course of twentieth-century history: had the troops at the Montaña Barracks sided immediately with Franco, they might have finished off the Second Republic in a matter of hours. The swift regime change which many expected would actually have happened and there would have been no civil war in Spain. Exactly how this would have altered Spanish and European history can only be guessed at, but both would certainly have looked very different. In the event, the barracks were the scene of a massacre which heralded much of the bloodletting to come.

Historically important maybe, but the city authorities in Madrid scarcely acknowledge the significance of what happened here. They certainly offer up no explanations. The main entrance to the park is dominated by a striking sculpture that represents both a prostrate body and a rifle surrounded by sandbags. There is more than a hint of violence and an inscription which reads: "1936 - a los Caídos en el Cuartel de la Montaña - 1972" (to the fallen in the Montaña Barracks). But there is no more information about why the sculpture is there or what it represents. Of the old barracks there remains not a trace, and about what happened to the garrison there in July 1936 not a word. Not surprisingly, most bewildered visitors simply press on, puzzled by the sculpture but none the wiser. Yet the story of what happened here is a fascinating tale and critical to understanding the history of Madrid in the Civil War. (1)

*

Few *Madrileños* were surprised when news reached the city, early on Saturday 18 July 1936, that part of the military high command had declared a *pronunciamiento* (military *coup*). Trouble had been brewing for months and was at fever pitch after a week of high-profile assassinations. The leaders of the *coup*, however, were all well outside Madrid, and whether their uprising succeeded or not would depend on reactions in Spain's main towns and cities. Most important of all was Madrid: if troops stationed in the capital joined the uprising, the Republic was effectively finished.

As the day wore on, the telegraph lines which connected Madrid to the rest of Spain clicked and crackled with the latest news. General Franco had been sprung from his base on the Canary Islands (in a clandestine operation involving Britain's MI6) and had rejoined the Spanish Legionaries in North Africa. The details, however, were sketchy while the immediate questions for the politicians in Madrid were stark: how much support did the rebels have? How many other officers were in on the conspiracy? How many troops would remain loyal to the Republic? And what would happen in Madrid?

The largest garrison in the capital was at the Montaña Barracks, situated on a promontory on the western side of the Plaza de España. The imposing three-story fortress, built in the 1860s, was a bastion for the defense of the city—a symbol of military clout. In a country where the democratic tradition and rule of constitutional law were weak, the barracks were a

The Montaña Barracks (private collection)

center of real power. Fully manned, they housed about 3,000 soldiers, although in mid-July many were on summer leave and the garrison was only at half strength. Even so, there would only be one outcome from a confrontation between disciplined, well-armed soldiers and the rag-bag of poorly supplied, untrained militia groups. Scores of these armed groups had been spawned by the different political parties and trade unions on the left to defend the Republic. Each was hell-bent on opposing the uprising but beyond that there was little coordination between them.

While ministers tried to make sense of the events unfolding around Spain, the left in Madrid was urging immediate action. Political groups—communists, anarchists, socialists—and trade unions urgently stepped up pressure on the government to arm citizens' militias to defend the Republic. Some ministers feared that with the situation spiraling out of control more armed, roving vigilante bands on the streets of Madrid would simply make matters worse. On the other hand, rightwing groups of monarchists and Falangists were already mobilizing to support the rebels. Earlier in the day, around 250 Falangists had slipped in to join the troops at the Montaña Barracks on the assumption that this would be the center of the uprising in Madrid. Some wore their trademark blue Falangist shirts while others were decked out in military kit and all were given weapons.

Throughout the turbulent weekend of 18-19 July the violence intensified. The government eventually and reluctantly agreed to distribute weapons but this decision, too, begged a question which could only be answered by the quartermaster of the garrison at the Montaña Barracks. Some 45,000 rifle bolts were stored in the building. Without these firing mechanisms many of the weapons being issued to pro-Republican militia groups were effectively useless. They looked like guns but without bolts might as well have been broomsticks. The garrison's commanders stalled for time and refused to hand over the bolts: while uncertain about joining the rebels, they also resisted arming the militia.

Prevarication over the rifle bolts merely heightened the popular clamor around the Monataña Barracks and emphasized the pivotal question: whose side was the garrison on? The conspirators had, of course, made plans to take control of the barracks—and the city—but these had been thwarted just days before the *coup* began. The plotters' link man in Madrid, Colonel Valentín Galarza, was a leader of the semi-secret, ultra-Nationalist officers' club the Unión Militar Española. Galarza, however, had been detained the previous week by police on well-founded suspicions of conspiring against the Republic. His number two in the plot had managed to give security forces the slip but he was now in hiding and unable to steer events. This course of events had left the conspirators without clear leadership in the capital: the commanders who remained at the Montaña were divided and confused about what to do next.

On the morning of Sunday 19 July the extreme rightwing General Joaquín Fanjul arrived at the Montaña. Fanjul was a man with form when it came to *coups*: he had taken a leading role in the failed *sanjurada* military uprising two years before and made little attempt to hide his contempt for the Republic. Fanjul immediately launched into an anti-Republican tirade before the assembled garrison and ordered leaflets to be printed on the barracks' presses. These proclaimed that the Spanish army was "prepared to save Spain from ignominy and put an end to government by assassins or international organizations." The general then declared a state of martial law in Madrid: all meetings and publications were banned and the city's "Marxist" trade unions dissolved. Fanjul demanded that workers maintain a "patriotic attitude" of obedience to the "Movement" which was about to "liberate" them.

Other officers, including the garrison's commander, expressed doubts either about the way events were unfolding or the capacity of the garrison to enforce martial law. Fanjul, however, presented the *coup* as a done deal. He insisted that troops stationed in Campamento and Carabanchel—districts to the south and west of the city—would join the rebellion and that more insurgent troops led by General Emilio Mola had already reached the mountains of the Sierra de Guadarrama. In fact, this was pure bluff. The mountains of the *sierra* offered Madrid natural protection and General Mola's advance ground to a halt in the face of fierce resistance by Republican militia in the tortuous mountain passes. Rebel troops never did break through the Republican defense, and they remained pinned down there for the next three years.

If Mola's reinforcements remained a distant mirage, those inside the building could both hear and see the throng of people who now surrounded the barracks. A hostile crowd, by now several hundred strong, spilled out from the Plaza de España up the Calle Ferraz and Paseo del Pintor Rosales. In a microcosm

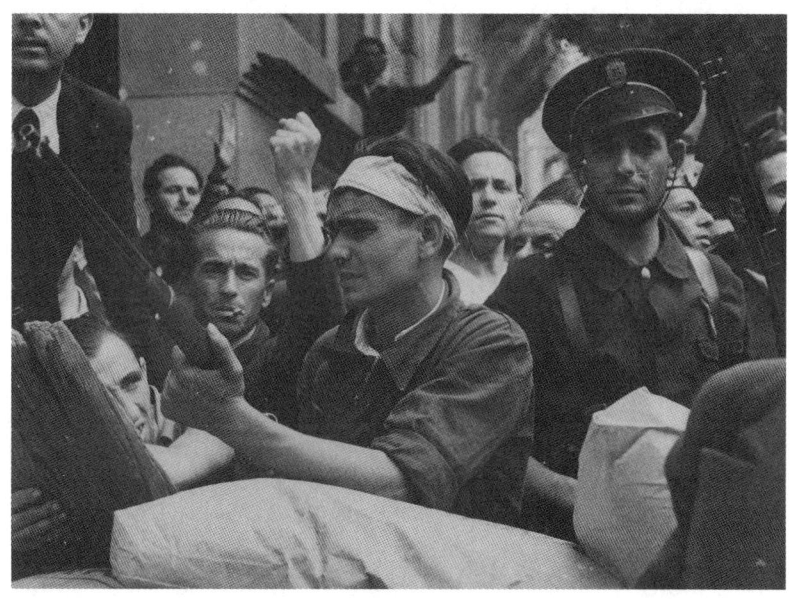

Militiamen in the Calle Luisa Fernanda opposite the Montaña Barracks, July 1936. (Ministerio de Educación, Cultura y Deporte, Archivo General de la Administración [Archivo Rojo])

of the disorganization that plagued the subsequent Republican war effort, the command center of the operation in the Plaza de España soon turned into a chaotic scene. Hundreds of sightseers turned up and mingled with the militia who were preparing to storm the barracks, and despite the efforts of the police, the pro-Republican military, and the Guardia Civil, it proved impossible to separate them from the fighters.

Meanwhile, inside the barracks the situation was less than clear cut. Fanjul's authority was challenged and the tension grew as officers argued between themselves about what to do—a critical discussion hampered by an almost total ignorance of what was happening elsewhere. Communication lines linking the garrison to the outside world had been cut by the government so that the troops were isolated and had little idea of what was happening in the rest of Spain. Despite Fanjul's promises, lookouts on the roof could see plumes of smoke from other parts of the city but no sign of reinforcements or relief. (2)

An essential element of any conspiracy is that plans are laid in secret, but this meant that few in the barracks had any inkling of who intended to join the rebellion and who would remain loyal to the Republic. It was little wonder that many of the officers inside the Montaña Barracks agonized. Intelligence on which to base a decision was poor while the stakes could not have been higher.

*

The commanders in the Montaña were not alone in their indecision. In León, another garrison town in the north of Spain, Captain Juan Rodríguez Lozano was wrestling with the same dilemma. Rodríguez opted to remain loyal to the Republic but the majority of his fellow officers took a different view and zealously joined in with the *coup*. After a summary court martial, Rodríguez was taken out and shot by firing squad. Just hours before his execution he wrote a letter to his wife in which he declared his enduring love for her and their children and explained why he had stuck by his oath of loyalty to the democratically elected Republican government.

Rodríguez would probably have been forgotten, along with thousands of other officers who faced the predicament, had his grandson, José Luís Rodríguez Zapatero, not become the Prime Minister of Spain almost 70 years later. When Zapatero was elected in 2004, his inaugural speech to the Spanish parliament included an extract from his grandfather's valedictory letter. The effect was electric and the Spanish right were enraged. The speech signaled that a new generation of the Spanish left—Zapatero was a youthful 43 years old—wanted to re-examine the country's painful past.

Crowds gather in the Calle Luisa Fernanda opposite the Montaña Barracks. The Café Viena is still there today (Ministerio de Educación, Cultura y Deporte, Archivo General de la Administración. [Archivo Rojo])

*

Outside the barracks the situation became tenser by the hour. On Sunday 19 July growing numbers of leftwing militiamen gathered in the surrounding streets—the Calle Ferraz, Calle Ventura Rodríguez, and Plaza de España. Every move in and out of the barracks was now closely watched. When a Falangist leader arrived and tried to enter the barracks he was challenged by the vigilantes. After an altercation the man fled to a nearby house opposite the barracks in the Calle Luisa Fernanda. He was subsequently hunted down and killed by the pursuing militiamen.

By midday, the Montaña Barracks had become *the* focal point of tension in the capital of a nation on the verge of civil war. In the few hundred square meters of what today looks like a peaceful park, the fate of Spain was about to be played out in the searing heat of the July sun. An armed band of tense and frustrated Republicans started to take pot-shots at the barracks from the slopes which lead down to the Manzanares river. A captain and a cadet in the building were wounded. The fire was returned. Armored cars carrying Assault Guards—a security force loyal to the Republic—arrived and parked in streets neighboring Calle Ferraz. A delivery lorry from the local brewery towed heavy artillery into the Plaza de España and another field gun was placed on San Vicente hill which rises up by the Royal Palace some 300 meters from the barracks. The gunners began to prepare their range finders to inflict maximum damage. Loudspeaker broadcasts exhorted the soldiers to remain loyal to the Republic. Leaflets were dropped on the building from Republican planes flying overhead. The message was reinforced by sharpshooters who took up positions in buildings overlooking the barracks. Likely escape routes—in the event of the soldiers attempting to make a run for it—were blocked by the vigilante groups who now erected barricades to close off surrounding streets. (3)

Armored cars opposite the Montaña Barracks on the corner of the Calle Ferraz and Plaza de España. (Ministerio de Educación, Cultura y Deporte, Archivo General de la Administración [Archivo Rojo])

The stand-off continued through the evening of 19 July and into the sultry, summer night. The street lamps outside the barracks remained unlit and from within the building there were only occasional flickers of light. The eerie tension around the barracks contrasted with febrile activity elsewhere in the city, however. News of the army's treachery in attempting a *coup* against the Republic triggered fury on the political left. The revolutionary forces which the government had been struggling for months to control now broke loose. That night, as the official forces of law and order disintegrated, political militia groups—in particular the communists—seized effective control of the city. A prime target was arguably the most conservative power in Spain, the Catholic hierarchy. Anti-clerical zealotry, never far from the surface of Republican Spain, swept the city. During that one night of rioting and looting alone some 50 churches were set ablaze. At the Church of San Fernando in the Lavapíes district, for example, there was a pitched battle between communists and Falangists as the church went up in flames: the shell of the building can still be seen today (see Chapter 3).

As the sun rose over Madrid on Monday 20 July 1936 it promised to be another blisteringly hot day—and a decisive one for the future of the Spanish Republic. General Fanjul still expected General Mola's army from Burgos to enter Madrid, join up with the garrison at the Montaña Barracks, and seal the success of the *coup*. But time went by and there was no sign of Mola or his men. Reports from elsewhere were confused and sketchy and merely added to the sense of crisis. Increasingly desperate, officers sympathetic to the rebels signaled from the roof of the Montaña Barracks to other troops in the southwestern outskirts of Madrid to come to their aid and lift the siege. They could not know it but these other barracks had already fallen into the hands of the Republican militia and the rebel commanders there were about to be shot. At 7AM the government made one last effort to negotiate the surrender of the Montaña garrison. An emissary carrying a white flag approached the main gate at the corner of the Calle Ferrraz and the Calle Luisa Fernanda. He apparently attempted to speak to General Fanjul and other officers but the exchange was brief and fruitless. The garrison commander claimed that his troops had done nothing disloyal to the Republic and that he could not understand why the barracks were being besieged. Under the circumstances it was an incredible lie. When the commander went on to demand that a van be allowed to pass through the militia cordon to collect the morning bread, Republican commanders replied that the troops had ten minutes to start evacuating the barracks, leaving five at a time.

This did not happen and Republican artillery began to

shell the garrison with a 155mm field gun at point blank range. Each round was applauded by the bystanders and a volley of shots from those militiamen who were lucky enough to have bolts in their rifles. Shortly before 10:30AM a white flag appeared from one of the windows of the barracks and drooped listlessly down the outside wall. It looked as though the garrison was about to give up. A group of militiamen jubilantly approached the main gates to the barracks but instead of taking the surrender they were met by a volley of fire. Several were killed outright and others badly wounded. Exactly how this came about has never been clarified. The fusillade came from windows away from the white flag and it seems likely that the shots were fired by other soldiers who never had any intention of surrendering. What happened next, however, is well documented. There was a full-scale massacre. Enraged Republican forces pounded the building with more artillery fire, breaching the walls at various points. Around 180 shells were fired in total with more 10-kilo bombs dropped by planes from the Republican-held airbase in Getafe on the southern outskirts of Madrid. Several assailants scaled the walls and entered the building through the roof. Others climbed through the holes left by the artillery fire and by late morning the militiamen had overwhelmed those inside. Some defenders tried to surrender and gave clenched fists salutes or shouted slogans about the Communist International.

But for many it was too late. The fury of the militia was sparked not just by the duplicity of the white flag, but by a deeper hatred directed at the institution of the military itself. The crowd storming the barracks turned into a lynch mob. Rookie cadets and experienced officers alike were herded onto the barrack square and machine gunned to death. Terrified officers who tried to hide in cupboards or under beds were shot or stabbed on the spot. Others were simply thrown out of the windows. Not surprisingly some officers preferred suicide to escape the carnage. Captain Orad de la Torre, a soldier who remained loyal to the Republic, walked into the barracks. Passing the NCO mess he saw a group of officers slumped around the table. "At the head was a major with a bullet hole through his heart; all the others were slumped with similar bullet holes. They had sat down there I suppose when they knew all was lost and the major had taken out his revolver and committed suicide; his junior officers followed his example." Torre recognized some of the dead "as brother-officers of mine."

What made the massacre so horrific was the random nature of the killing. Some of the Republic's professional soldiers or more disciplined Assault Guard accepted the surrender of fellow officers, laughing with and even embracing those inside. Yet in other parts of the building the assailants gave no quarter. For many soldiers in the Montaña Barracks, their fate depended on the character of the militiamen who found them first rather than any notion of justice. It was a grim foretaste of what would follow in the Civil War over the next three years.

And what became of the conspirator in chief, General Fanjul? Although wounded by shrapnel from the bombing, he was identified almost immediately and taken off by Republican Assault Guards to the State Security department. There he was tried on charges of treason and inciting rebellion. He was found guilty and on 14 August 1936 Fanjul was executed by firing squad on a spot not far from the Montaña Barracks.

The remainder of the surviving troops suspected of having any sympathy with the rebel generals were thrown into the nearby Cárcel Modelo (Model Prison) at the Plaza Moncloa, about ten minutes' walk from the Montaña Barracks. As it turned out this was merely a reprieve and by the end of the year most of them would be dead too, victims of another massacre. In November 1936 the rebel army laid siege to Madrid and the Model Prison was on the front line. Thousands of political prisoners there, including those from the Montaña Barracks, were loaded into trucks destined, apparently, for Valencia on the Mediterranean coast and well away from Madrid. They never arrived. At a small village called Paracuellos some 20 kilometers outside Madrid and close to what is now Barajas International Airport, the convoy came to a halt. The prisoners were ordered down from the trucks and executed by machine gunners. It was one of the most callous acts of a war stained by atrocities.

And the Montaña Barracks? The Civil War had still not finished with them. The generals' *coup* failed to topple the Republic within a matter of hours and deliver the expected swift regime change—not least because the garrison at the Montaña failed to join the rebel forces. Spain was plunged into bloody internecine strife. By November 1936 the Nationalist army had marched up through the south of Spain and was at the gates of Madrid, ready to take the city through the open parkland known as the Casa de Campo on the western side. The hollow shell of the barracks was now on the new frontline of the besieged city. During the course of the siege, what was left was shelled to rubble. After the war the ground was cleared and used for soccer fields in the 1950s and 1960s. The only image of the barracks which remains on public view is an old sepia photograph of the site now stuck incongruously on top of a circular public toilet between the park and Paseo del Pintor Rosales.

In 1972 the area was remodeled. An elegant Egyptian temple, the Templo de Debod, now dominates the center of the new park (4). This building was saved from the rising waters of the River Nile when the Aswan Dam was constructed in the 1960s. It was then presented by the Egyptian government to Madrid by way of thanks for the assistance lent by Spanish engineers in the project. There is plenty of information about the temple constructed on another continent in a different millennium, and it is well worth a visit. But about the deadly events which took place in this same park some 80 years ago there is nothing but an enigmatic sculpture and one faded photograph on a toilet. (5)

Tour Details (See Area map on p. 103)

Directions: The main entrance to the Templo Debod part of Parque del Oeste is across Calle Ferraz from Plaza de España (Metro: Plaza de España).

Duration: 1 Hour

(1) A double flight of steps leads up to the park and the temple; these correspond with the original staircases which led to the main entrance of the barracks in 1936. Today there is a sculpture of a fallen soldier surrounded by stone sandbags between the staircases, whereas in 1936 there was a simple retaining wall.

A viewpoint behind the Egyptian temple has stunning views over the Casa de Campo to the mountains of the Sierra de Guadarrama beyond. This is an excellent place from which

Memorial "to the fallen of the Montaña Barracks" at the entrance to the Templo Debod. (James Ferguson)

to understand the events at the barracks—and the course of the siege of Madrid. To the northwest (on the right hand side) are the mountains through which the Nationalist officers at the barracks hoped that General Mola's relief column would arrive in July 1936. To the southwest (on the left hand side) are the districts of Campamento and Carabanchel. Observers on the roof of the Montaña kept a look out for signals from other barracks located in these districts.

The nearby Royal Palace was, of course, occupied by the President of the Republic in 1936.

The Egyptian temple dominates the center of the park today and occupies a part of the site on which the Montaña Barracks stood in 1936.

The circular, unisex pay toilet, with only visual reference to the Montaña Barracks, is on the pavement between the park and the Paseo del Pintor Rosales.

5

MADRID'S WESTERN FRONT: THE CASA DE CAMPO, PARQUE DEL OESTE, AND UNIVERSITY CAMPUS

> "Madrid, Madrid; how good your name sounds,
> breakwater for all the Spains!
> The earth shatters, the sky thunders,
> you smile with a leaden heart."
> Antonio Machado, 7 November 1936

In the late autumn of 1936 a small group of students were sitting quietly in the university library perusing piles of books. John Cornford, already a published poet who had just graduated from Cambridge, held out a volume and commented to his friends that it was "rather good history." Before any of the others could reply, the students were knocked off their feet by a massive explosion. Cornford remained unconscious where he fell, with blood gushing from his head, while the others struggled through thick black smoke and rubble to take up their positions by the reading room windows. General Franco's Nationalist army was on the attack—and the students were right in the line of fire.

Following their botched *coup* of July 1936 the rebel generals embarked on a campaign to take control of Spain city by city. By November Franco's Army of Africa was closing in on Madrid. In July ordinary *Madrileños* had stifled the original *coup* attempt in Madrid at the Montaña Barracks. Now they prepared to defend their city again. Under the famous slogan of *No Pasarán* the citizens of Madrid were joined in their struggle by thousands of volunteers in the International Brigades. The volunteers came from some fifty different countries and the twenty-year-old John Cornford was one of them.

This chapter (and the Route below) follows in the footsteps of the International Brigades along a two-kilometer stretch of the old frontline. Some of the bloodiest fighting of the entire Civil War took place here: in the Casa de Campo, across the River Manzanares, through the Parque del Oeste, and on the university campus. By 1939 the whole area looked like a sector of the Western Front during World War I, following a particularly bloody exchange. This chapter will seek to explain how events unfolded in the two decisive weeks from 8-22 November 1936 when the Nationalist army attempted to storm Madrid—and the Republicans fought tooth and nail to stop them.

The attempted *coup* of 18 July 1936 failed in Madrid, but some parts of Spain were quickly under rebel control and the conspirators had no intention of giving up. They soon put together plans for a military campaign to conquer the capital and topple the Republic. While rebel troops could not break through the mountains to the north of Madrid, General Franco's army rolled remorselessly up through the south and west of Spain towards the capital. The Republicans calculated that the final stage of Franco's assault on Madrid would be determined by the city's unusual layout. The center of old Madrid is dominated by the Royal Palace, built on an escarpment by the Bourbons in the eighteenth century. A huge tract of woodland known as the Casa de Campo (literally "country house") fans out from the palace to the west. The parkland continues almost without interruption to the mountains of the Sierra de Guadarrama on the horizon and the impression given is of open countryside rolling right into the center of the city. Much of the Casa de Campo was acquired for use as a hunting ground by the Habsburg King Felipe II in the sixteenth century, and during the next three hundred years it was used exclusively for royal pleasure. Then, when the monarchy collapsed in 1931 and King Alfonso XIII fled the country, the new Republican government immediately opened up the Casa de Campo as a public space accessible to all.

Today, watching the sun set over the Casa de Campo and the *sierra* beyond is one of Madrid's better-known pleasures. Less well advertised is the role that the area played during the siege of Madrid. The undulating pinewoods and hillocks of the parkland were converted into killing fields when both sides were locked in battle along Madrid's western front. (1) As the struggle for control of the area intensified, the armies built up an elaborate network of trenches and fortifications. Most of the woodland flora and fauna was blown away by crossfire and when the war ended in 1939 the parkland was littered with huge quantities of highly unstable ordnance. The clean-up took years, and it was only considered safe enough to start re-opening some areas to the public in 1947. Even today the most stubborn military relics in the Casa de Campo and adjoining Parque del Oeste (West Park) remain firmly in their place. There is, however, little public information offered about the history of the area or why the remains are there. (2)

On 6 November 1936 Nationalist troops entered the Casa de Campo at the western end and moved swiftly east toward the city center. Hardly anyone expected Madrid to survive the attack. The few foreign journalists left in the city met in a bar to swap notes and discuss the situation. They organized a "guess how long it will take Madrid to fall" competition, and each wrote down the time which they thought would elapse before the first rebel troops came marching up the street. Estimates ranged from hours to a few days. Only one wrote "never," just to be different. Some of those reporters were subsequently left red-faced by filing stories which actually recounted the fall of Madrid—one complete with the colorful description of a dog supposedly yapping at the heels of the Nationalist troops as they paraded through the city center.

Not far away, government ministers too were meeting and reached conclusions identical to those of the foreign correspondents: they decided that Madrid's position was untenable and that they should leave at once to establish a new seat of government in Valencia on the Mediterranean coast. With that, the entire government led by Prime Minister Largo Caballero fled the city.

Flight was a craven response not open to most *Madrileños,* although there was good reason for many to be alarmed at the approach of Franco's columns. A large contingent of the rebel forces came from the Army of Africa, based in Morocco, and these troops had a track record of cold-blooded savagery. The vanguard of the African Army came from the crack Spanish Legion. Known as the Bridegrooms of Death, their organizing principle was terror and their battle cry *Viva La Muerte!* (Long Live Death) may sound absurd, but only at a distance. Airlifted from Morocco on planes lent by Hitler, the Army of Africa had slashed and burned its way up from the south of Spain towards Madrid. The novelist Arthur Koestler, then a journalist in Spain, described how "the shadows of the Middle Ages seemed to have come alive with gargoyles spouting blood... the Foreign Legionaries killed, raped, and plundered in the name of a holy crusade, while the air smelt of incense and burning flesh."

Refugees fleeing from their path arrived in the capital to tell of the atrocities which had been committed. The most infamous example of all took place in Badajoz, a provincial town in the Extremadura region to the west of Spain. The citizens of Badajoz had attempted to defend their town but were soon overrun by rebel troops. The Nationalist soldiers swaggered through the streets ripping the shirts of the townspeople to identify those who had resisted—a shoulder bruised by the recoil of a rifle was the tell-tale sign. Suspects, about 2,000 in all, were rounded up and held in the bullring where they were then machine gunned to death in small groups. A shocked Portuguese journalist went over the border to investigate the story and confronted the officer in charge, General Yagüe. "Two thousand," shrugged the general, "no, no I don't think it was that many." Yagüe defended his action indignantly to another journalist: "what did people expect me to do—keep thousands of *Rojo* (Red) prisoners who could later attack my columns from the rear?" Many in Madrid expected a similar fate if the Nationalists took control of the capital. "It is necessary to spread terror," said one of Franco's senior commanders. "We have to create the impression of mastery, eliminating without scruples or hesitation all those who do not think as we do." Foreign journalists were taken aback when a Nationalist press attaché mused that it might be necessary to execute up to 50,000 *Madrileños.*

Responsibility for the defense of Madrid now passed to two army generals who had stayed loyal to the Republic. General José Miaja was left to organize the defense of the city itself whilst General Sebastián Pozas took command of the Army of the Center, which controlled the large area to the east of the city. Just moments before he left for Valencia, Prime Minister Largo Caballero handed the generals sealed orders and insisted that they should only be opened at the respective divisional headquarters the following morning. It was a bizarre instruction—and promptly ignored. Miaja and Pozas ripped open the envelopes to discover that each had been given the orders meant for the other. Whether this was mere bungling or an attempt by a Nationalist "mole" to sabotage the defense of the city from the top down has never been explained. The sure fact is that had the generals not acted on their own initiative and untangled the confusion, Madrid would have been in an even more precarious position. Yet even with the right plans, Miaja's position looked grim, and he knew that a successful defense of Madrid would only be possible with the full support of all the pro-Republican forces in the city.

Given the chaos and political infighting which had gone on since the summer, instilling discipline was no easy task: as Miaja's highly able second in command, Colonel Vicente Rojo, commented wryly: "we had one day to remake everything that we had spent the previous five months unmaking."

Miaja well understood that he was being set up to take the blame for the expected defeat but nevertheless set about imposing order on the bickering factions. In this he was aided principally by the Communist Party, which flooded the city with revolutionary propaganda and slogans:

> Madrid Will be the Tomb of Fascism
> *¡No Pasarán!*
> Every house a fortress, every street a trench, every neighborhood a wall of iron and combatants...
> ¡Emulate Petrograd: 7 November on the Manzanares must be as glorious as on the Neva!
> Viva Madrid without a Government

One activist recalled that the phrase *No Pasarán* was repeated endlessly during the following days. "It was like an advertisement which says 'use instant shaving cream' and you do. Everyone believed it..."

In fact, Republican militiamen were already putting up stiff resistance in the Casa de Campo to stem the Nationalist onslaught. The rebel advance was eventually slowed about 100 meters from the large ornamental boating lake near what is now the Madrid Zoo. Today the lake is surrounded by lively open air bars and restaurants but in November 1936 the area was a killing field. (3)

The most advanced Nationalist forces occupied several of the small hillocks near the lake. These overlooked the Manzanares river on the other side. The Nationalists also managed to seize the highest hill in the Casa de Campo, known as Cerro Garabitas (Garabitas Hill). With clear views over the whole of Madrid, this was a vital strategic vantage point for the rebels' heavy artillery and, despite several savage counterattacks, the Republicans were unable to dislodge them. *Madrileños* were tormented relentlessly by the guns on Garabitas Hill, and one resident compared the hill to a volcano which "shook and smoked" for most of the war. Today a cable car runs into this section of the Casa de Campo from Parque del Oeste. The ride gives a panoramic view over the battlefield, and the cable car station in Casa de Campo is very close to the Nationalist gunners' positions in 1936. (4)

By 8 November the Nationalist army had edged closer to the banks of the Manzanares river along a stretch between the Puente de los Franceses (French Bridge), a railway viaduct, and the Puente del Rey (King's Bridge). (5, 6) For the next week the battle for Madrid was fought out along this section of the waterway, and it became the most deadly sector of the city's western front. The river runs slowly down the western side of Madrid between the Casa de Campo and the city itself. The Manzanares is not wide, but nevertheless presented an important natural barrier and was crucial to the Republican defense of the city. Beyond the river on the city side the ground rises steeply into the Parque del Oeste, and this too was a key element of Republican defensive tactics. The combination of a river and rising ground on the opposite bank was a serious hurdle for Nationalist assault troops to overcome. (7)

The militias dug in furiously along the Parque del Oeste to build better defenses against the expected attack, though one combatant recalled that some trenches "were little more than ditches." He arrived at the park and was told, "here is the trench, get in it, we have got to defend this." He was handed a dirty Italian rifle which he set about cleaning with a tin of Nivea cream, kept from an outing to the *sierra* before the war.

On 8 November Republican defiance was further boosted by the arrival of around 2,500 volunteers from the International Brigade at Atocha Railway Station (see Chapter 3). The volunteers marched in formation through the city and down the Gran Vía

Digging the defenses: trenches stretched across Parque del Oeste and the university campus. (Google Art Project)

to the Plaza de España where they split into three battalions. The first went up the Calle Princesa to the university while the second went to Paseo del Pintor Rosales and Parque del Oeste, and the third down the San Vicente hill to the Casa de Campo. Before crossing the river, this third group again mustered in the yard of the Estación del Norte or North Station. (8)

The brigade in Madrid was commanded by Manfred Stern, a Jewish Ukrainian medical student and better known by his *nom de guerre* "General Kléber" (one of Napoleon's commanders). To avoid the prohibitions of the Non-Intervention Agreement, Stern had entered Spain disguised as a furrier—an implausible guise during the sweltering heat of September. Stern was a natural, if hard, leader who made such a success of his command in November

1936 that he became known as the "saviour of Madrid." Whether deserved or not, the adulation was too much for the paranoid Stalin. Stern was recalled to Moscow. After a summary trial in May 1939, he was sentenced to 15 years hard labor in Siberia but never completed the term, dying in his gulag in 1954.

On 9 November there was a brief rebel incursion across the Manzanares. A small contingent of Nationalist troops advanced as far as the junction of Calle Marqués de Urquijo and Paseo del Pintor Rosales, but met with stiff resistance. Barricades had been erected across the streets leading down to the park and resistance in the area was bolstered by the newly arrived volunteers of the International Brigade. (9) By the end of the day the assault had been beaten back across the river.

Clearly the Nationalists needed to mount a more robust offensive on Madrid but the options were limited. With just 18,000 troops at his disposal, the Nationalist general in overall command of the assault, Enrique Varela, was short of firepower and there were no available reinforcements. Varela could not call on troops from the north or south of the line without leaving his flanks exposed and vulnerable to a Republican counterattack; a Republican pincer movement might encircle the troops in the Casa de Campo leaving the main force surrounded.

On the Republican side, the western front of Madrid was heavily defended by around 25,000 men and women. They were mainly civilian members of militias mixed with professional soldiers who had remained loyal to the Republic. Loudspeaker vans toured the city, noisily appealing for extra volunteers to bolster the defense forces. Volunteers also arrived from outside Madrid. Apart from the volunteers of the International Brigades, 3,000 anarchist militiamen arrived from the Catalonia front and their presence, too, boosted morale in the city. Although the numbers of combatants were tipped—just—in favor of the Republicans, the rebels had the advantage in terms of equipment and supplies. Shortages of matériel and poor distribution hampered the Republican war effort throughout the conflict, despite Soviet support, and at times the position in Madrid was dire. One commander, for example, was forced to leave stockpiles of shells at intervals along the River Manzanares and tow the three or four cannons he could find along the banks. His crew then fired a few rounds from each of the small ammunition dumps, trying to give an impression of defenses more robust than they really were.

Between 8 and 15 November the two sides slogged it out through the Casa de Campo and along the banks of the Manzanares. Fighting was particularly savage around the partly blown Puente Nuevo (New Bridge) and adjacent Puente de los Franceses. Time and again the Nationalists charged the bridges with everything they had—tanks, armored cars, and infantry—in an attempt to cross the river. A message was sent to the commander of the embattled Republican troops on the bridge asking if his men needed reinforcements. "Just send us more grenades," he replied. (10)

But as the days went on, bravura could not disguise the fact that the troops on both sides were exhausted. Constant bombing and night attacks left many of the Republicans with little more than a few hours sleep. Colonel Rojo later commented, "in those first days of the battle nobody—either in the HQ or on the front—could sleep more than a couple of hours because the combat was unremitting and implacable and we thought that at any moment we could be overtaken by a decisive crisis." On the Nationalist side, troops were already worn down by the incessant fighting during their long campaign through southern Spain. They had expected a quick victory in Madrid, but it was not happening and they were exasperated.

14 November was a cold, damp autumn day. The mist along the river was punctuated by the crackle of rifle fire and the occasional rattle of machine guns strafing enemy lines. At the Nationalist field HQ in the Casa de Campo, General Varela convened a meeting of his senior commanders. Rebel troops had advanced to the banks of the Manzanares upstream, to the

The carefully landscaped Parque del Oeste soon looked more like a sector of the Western Front during World War I. (Biblioteca Nacional de España, fondo fotográfico de la guerra civil española)

north of the Puente de los Franceses, and Varela's officers now weighed up the chances of launching a fresh attack across the river there. Those gathered around the table knew that the attack would be highly dangerous; the sector was well covered by Republicans on the opposite bank and from the heights of the Puente de los Franceses. It was not an easy call, and opinions were divided. General Yagüe, who had ordered the slaughter of Republican prisoners in Badajoz, was the officer in charge of that sector of the line. Yagüe vehemently opposed what he described as a suicidal assault and then, in an indication of the fatigue and stress now being felt on both sides, he fainted. But Colonel Asensio, one of the officers designated to lead the charge, insisted the attack would make it. "Tomorrow," he bragged, "I am going to cross the river—come what may." And it was this view that carried the day.

At 9AM on 15 November, an intense artillery barrage pummeled the Republican defenses along the river for an hour. An hour later, Nationalists launched a fresh assault on the Puente de los Franceses and Puente Nuevo. Some 6,000 soldiers in three columns, with artillery and air support, were engaged in the attack. The troops were led in the field by commanders Asensio, Barrón, and Delgado Serrano. The plan of attack was to take the Puente de los Franceses and the remains of the Puente Nuevo. Once across the river, the three columns would head up the rising ground on the opposite bank and fan out. Colonel Asensio would lead his column to capture objectives in the university campus on the left flank, while Delgado Serrano would move up the slopes of the Parque del Oeste in the center to take the Cárcel Modelo and adjacent Infante San Juan Barracks on the edge of the park. (11) Finally, Barrón would take the right flank, moving up onto Paseo del Pintor Rosales, the Montaña Barracks, and Plaza de España. (12)

Seizing the Model Prison was of particular importance to Nationalists, who believed that hundreds of rightwing political prisoners were being held there. They were mistaken. The authorities in Madrid had already begun an extensive program of *sacas* (removals) throughout November. Prisoners were taken by trucks away from the possible battlegrounds, supposedly to safe havens. Many never arrived (see Chapter 4).

By 10:30AM on 15 November, Nationalist tanks were in advanced positions and within yards of securing the bridges. The Republicans threw in everything they had to defend the crossings—reinforcements were rapidly drafted in to shore up defenses, and the tanks were repelled only at the last moment. The combat that morning cost the Republicans dearly, but the attack was again thwarted. It was the closest the Nationalists ever came to taking the bridges, which remained in Republican hands for the rest of the war.

The rebels had greater success some 700 meters upriver from the Puente de los Franceses. Here the perimeter of the Casa de

Campo was divided from the Manzanares by a wall designed in Italianate style by the eighteenth-century court architect Francesco Sabatini. Nationalist artillery blew a four-meter wide hole through the elegant brickwork before tanks and armored cars trundled through the gap in what soon became a chaotic advance. The heavy-plated armored vehicles floundered in the mud. The infantry could not cross the river without support, so the assault troops were left exposed on the river bank and at the mercy of the increasing incoming fire from the other side.

By mid-afternoon the only viable strategy appeared to be retreat, but with a last throw of the dice the Nationalists gambled on a unit of highly experienced Moroccan soldiers. They were led by Mohammed ben Mizzian, the most senior Moroccan officer in the Nationalist army and a devout Muslim who had once saved Franco's life during a skirmish with tribesmen from the Rif. At around 4PM, under cover of tank fire, ben Mizzian's men somehow managed to wade across the river and establish a foothold on the eastern bank. The Republican militia now retreated in panic while the jubilant Nationalist troops surged up the hill toward the university. Mohammed ben Mizzian was wounded in the pursuit but recovered sufficiently to join his men later in the year—and then go on to become defense minister of the newly independent Morocco in the 1960s.

Crossing the river was a crucial gain for the Nationalists, and the focus of the battle for Madrid now shifted to the university campus. The plan for a grandiose university city on a green-field site just outside the city originated with General Miguel Primo de Rivera, who governed Spain from 1923 to 1930. Primo was a bluff, rotund dictator known as the "Spanish Mussolini." Intolerant of political opposition, he nevertheless understood that the country needed to modernize, and the new unified campus for Madrid's University, called the Complutense, was part of his grand plan to kick Spain into the twentieth century. In 1936 the project was still being completed. Some—but not all—of the science buildings were equipped while other faculties were still being furnished and libraries installed. When students and staff broke for the summer vacation in June 1936, it was the last time that many of them would ever set foot on the campus.

One academic was a young head archivist, Juana Capdevielle. She worked at the library in the Faculty of Philosophy and Letters where John Cornford and others from the International Brigades were later holed up. Within a few weeks the Civil War would turn Juana's life on its head—and then end it. Fulfilled in her work—she had overseen the removal of 150,000 volumes to the new faculty library—Juana married a young Complutense law professor, Francisco ("Paco") Pérez Carballo, in March 1936. The following month Francisco was appointed to the administrative post of Civil Governor in the northwestern town of La Coruña. When news of the uprising reached the town on 20 July, there was pandemonium. The Military Governor of the local garrison assured Francisco that his troops would not join the rebellion. On the basis of that promise, Francisco refused to release weapons to the local trade unions which were clamoring for arms to defend the Republic. It was a fatal mistake. Other officers in the garrison detained their commander and then went for Francisco. Both were given a summary trial and executed on the spot. A few minutes before his execution Francisco wrote the following note from his cell:

> Juana
> You have been the most beautiful thing in my life. Wherever you are and while I can think, I will think of you. It will be as though we are together. I kiss the ring you gave me every day. I love you. Paco
>
> Friday, 24 July, 1936, at 5AM

But Juana may never have read Paco's note because she was already on the run. Captured and imprisoned, she lost the baby she was expecting. On 18 August Juana was released from her cell. Desperate, she sought refuge in the house of a local politician but a Falangist hit squad hunted her down. The next day Juana's raped and murdered corpse was found in a ditch by the main road out of the town.

*

As Spain spiraled into civil war over the summer of 1936, thousands of other lives were also in turmoil. At the university, letters were sent out to students warning them that the start of the new term would be delayed "until further notice." In the event, the Complutense campus was one of the most fiercely contested theaters of the conflict. Faculty buildings where it was intended to promote a deeper understanding of Western culture became scenes of barbarism. The Russian correspondent for *Pravda*, Mikhail Koltsov, wondered in his diary, "who would have thought that the most scientific, academic, and organized corner of Madrid would become the scene of the most bloody and violent combat?" In particular, the university's *clínico*, dedicated to healing the sick, became a death trap.

About 800 meters directly up the slope towards the university, Nationalist troops were held off briefly at the Faculty of Architecture and the Casa Velázquez—both buildings were wrecked in a few hours. The imposing cultural center of Casa Velázquez was built in the 1920s on the spot where the famous painter had made sketches of the Guadarrama mountains for use as background in some of his finest work. It was defended, room by room, by Hungarians from the International Brigade who were killed to the last man. Then the Nationalist troops surged across the Coruña Road, the principal road from Madrid to Galicia in the northwest of Spain, where they also took the Faculty of Agriculture after a fierce struggle. (13)

By late evening of 15 November the Nationalists had some 500 troops on the Madrid side of the River Manzanares.

The Casa Velázquez, center, and Faculty of Architecture, right (Biblioteca Nacional de España, fondo fotográfico de la guerra civil española)

During the night they consolidated their gains, and engineers constructed a wooden causeway across the river about 400 meters north of the Puente de los Franceses. This bridge was the essential link in the supply line of food, water, and munitions to the rebel troops now on the university campus. Naturally, it was a target for Republican artillery and air attacks. The crossing was destroyed about twenty times, according to one Nationalist engineer, but each time rebuilt, and every new version was more robust than the last. By the end of the war it was a solid structure with concrete sides to protect those crossing it from sniper fire. Nevertheless, the bridge amply deserved the name by which it was popularly known: *la pasarela de la muerte* (the gangway of death). (14) Entering or leaving the sector was normally only possible under cover of darkness, and the bridge remained the sole—and lethal—point of access for Nationalist supplies and troops. At times Republican attacks were so fierce that the bridge became unusable and it was only possible to drop provisions from the air. This too was a hazardous task under fire—as was collecting the dropped supplies from no-man's land.

The breach of the river defense and losses of 15 November could hardly have been more serious for the Republicans. They were now within a few streets of surrendering control of Madrid. Worse still, the militia had panicked under fire. As the professional soldiers leading the Republicans well knew, morale and discipline were vital to the defense of the city; panic, on the other hand, would be contagious.

At dawn on 16 November 1936 the fate of Madrid hung in the balance. Under a gray, somber sky, *Madrileños* had no idea

The *pasarela de la muerte* was constantly attacked and rebuilt during the course of the siege. (Ministerio de Educación, Cultura y Deporte, Archivo General de la Administración [Archivo Rojo])

whether this would be the day that their city fell to Franco. Prime Minister Largo Caballero, who had fled with the rest of the government to Valencia ten days before, tried to put a brave face on events. With a mixture of understatement and disingenuousness, he argued that "Madrid is not a favorable position militarily and in the hypothetical case that the fascists take control it would not be a moral loss." Throughout 16 November there was ceaseless, savage fighting across the university campus as Nationalists pushed up towards the streets of Madrid, faculty by faculty. But hundreds more Republican volunteers were flooding into the sector and pushing them back. The rebel advance was eventually checked in the main square of the university where the Republicans held on to the Faculties of Medicine (in the center) and Pharmacy (on the left). The ferocity of the fighting can be measured by the deep pockmarks of bullets and shrapnel which even today scar the buildings. (15)

Behind the lines—during breaks in the clouds—Nationalist bombers stepped up their campaign to harass the city: it was the most intense wave of air raids against a civilian population yet seen in the history of warfare. A 500-kilo bomb which fell in Puerta del Sol blew a vast hole and killed dozens of people (see Chapter 3). In the words of the correspondent for *Paris Soir* magazine, the attacks were "methodical slaughter". Yet—as with the Blitz in London four years later—these raids bred a mood of hatred and defiance towards the aggressors. *Madrileños* were terrified but in no mood to capitulate without a fight.

The vicious fighting and the bombing spilled over to the following day, the 17 November. The rebels had completed the crucial initial step of crossing the Manzanares river, but had still not met their key objectives. They had not been able to advance across the Parque del Oeste or liberate the political prisoners they believed were held in the Model Prison. Nor had they reached the adjacent Infante San Juan Barracks. Colonel Asenio had fulfilled his boast to cross the Manzanares "come what may," but his column could make no progress along Paseo del Pintor Rosales to the Montaña Barracks or Plaza de España. In short, the Nationalists were a few hundred meters closer to the center of Madrid but unable to seize control.

The Parque del Oeste and university campus in particular became muddy, bloody fields of close combat fighting, and the casualties on both sides were very heavy. Republican commanders Miaja and Rojo went to visit the Model Prison on the edge of the park. The jail was on the front line and directly overlooked the battle zone. The two commanders hoped to get a clearer idea of exactly what was happening from the observation point on the roof of the prison, but the unremitting bombardment shook the metal stairs so violently that they could not climb up. At ground level the battle raged without mercy on either side. When Miaja and Rojo tried to leave the prison through the Plaza de Moncloa, they ran into anarchist militiamen in full, chaotic retreat after a brutal Nationalist charge through the adjacent park. The majority were simply running for their lives but a few of the militia were trying to mount a rearguard action with machine guns. One recalled the moment saying, "more than being effective or getting the aim right we were just praying to all the saints that our gun did not jam." Pistol in hand, Miaja took charge. With bullets whistling around him Miaja set off, striding past the men and towards the line of fire, bawling orders, curses, and encouragement. It worked. The militiamen regained some of their courage and followed the general. Another Nationalist assault was held. The story was similar across the university sector. Republican soldiers were everywhere fighting with extraordinary resilience and stalling the rebel advance. Still more fresh units, including volunteers from the International Brigades, were being drafted in to shore up the defenses in the faculty buildings. From the air, Soviet Polikarpov 1-15 planes strafed Nationalist positions.

The next few days (17-22 November) were crucial in the siege of Madrid. In his memoirs, the Republican commander Vicente Rojo wrote of "the tension right along the front during those days… night and day Madrid was a hell of fire and destruction." The Nationalists' advance now meant that they occupied an area of the University City of about one square kilometer. To the north, the Nationalists held the Palacio de la Moncloa which can be seen from the A6 road (it is now the official residence of the Spanish Prime Minister and access is restricted). The frontline then stretched east through the university campus and round to the edge of Parque del Oeste in the south.

But while the Nationalists had gained ground, they were unable to progress further. They had established a salient but little if any advantage because they were now surrounded and attacked on three sides. Militarily, the most sensible option would have been a tactical withdrawal back over the river but this would have meant a loss of face: for General Franco, retreat was simply unthinkable.

The fighting was bitter but neither side could make a decisive breakthrough. When he first arrived on the university campus John Cornford had described the surrounding landscape as "rather Sussexy." By now it looked like one of the more contested sectors of the Western Front. The university grounds became an inferno. One combatant remembered that "we started a ruthless fight for every path, every house, every floor, every threshold. Here the front line goes through the most valuable laboratories and libraries." Faculty buildings changed hands hourly in the ferocious hand to hand combat. Each building was besieged by one side or the other. The military historian Antony Beevor has described the bitter fighting as "a foretaste of Stalingrad." John Whittaker was an American journalist "embedded" with Franco's army. He observed the "calm and methodical" Moroccan troops at work. They would surround a building and clear the ground floor resistance. Then, with automatic weapons and grenades, they worked their way up clearing each floor. "There was only one problem," noted Whittaker, "by the time the Moors reached the top floor there were no Moors left."

The vanguard of the rebel forces now reached the hospital

(now Hospital Clínico Universitario San Carlos) and a small chapel on the hillside called Santa Cristina. (The Santa Cristina was destroyed in the war and the Museo de América now stands on the site.) The hospital in particular was of tremendous strategic importance. Situated on high ground, its tall buildings, still under construction, offered a panoramic view over the whole front—from the university campus to the Casa de Campo. The other side looked out over Madrid, the buzzing streets and cafés of the city just a few hundred meters away.

It was ironic that a building designed to preserve life should become a tomb for many combatants. Fighting took place from room to room and floor to floor with bayonets and grenades. One technique, favored by both sides, was to knock a small hole in a wall, push a machine gun barrel though the gap and open fire. In the early stages of the battle, it was said that a grenade was placed in a lift. The lift was sent up to the floor above occupied by rebels where the grenade exploded, killing those who opened the door. (16)

The battle also continued underground and, like buildings in other parts of the sector, the hospital was extensively damaged by mines. In 1934 General Franco had been sent to the northern Spanish province of Asturias to put down a strike by miners in the region (see Chapter 1). This he did with great brutality—some 2,000 people were killed or wounded—and the miners now took their revenge on Franco's rebel forces. Asturian miners used their expertise to excavate into the sewerage ducts, and dug tunnels into the hillside under the hospital. These were then packed with dynamite. Those inside the building could hear the excavation work beneath their feet but had no idea where or when the explosion would be detonated. When the eruption finally came, sections of the building collapsed, burying the men inside under tons of concrete. Father Caballero, chaplain to a Nationalist division, described the aftermath of one explosion which brought down an operating theater where a company of men had been sheltering: "there was a lot of smoke. It was impossible to dig through the huge piles of rubble and twisted metal... also we were under fire now from the enemy. A wall collapsed and buried two more engineers who were involved in the rescue work. After an hour the men were found and some pulled out... I gave the absolution to them all."

Elsewhere on the university campus, volunteers from the XI International Brigade were also fighting for their lives. The Franco-Belgian Battalion, which included John Cornford and the other Cambridge students, were locked into a savage battle for control of the Faculty of Philosophy and Letters. (17) The building was initially held by the Republicans as a command post and field hospital, but they were overwhelmed by Nationalist troops and dislodged. International Brigade volunteers then managed to re-take the building in a battle fought with rifles, bayonets, and grenades. According to one participant, blood

The Faculty of Philosophy and Letters. The library held by John Cornford and the International Brigades is on the ground floor. (Biblioteca Nacional de España, fondo fotográfico de la guerra civil española)

ran down the stairs from the dead and wounded strewn about on every floor of the faculty. The volunteers held the faculty, but from then on were under permanent attack from the experienced, professional troops of the rebel army.

The volunteers fighting in the university at that point included an unusually high number of published writers: Germans Gustav Regler and Ludwig Renn and the Hungarian Mate Zalka, all novelists, fought alongside authors John Sommerfield, Bernard Knox, and John Cornford; the Pulitzer Prize-winning novelist Upton Sinclair described the group as "the most literary brigade in history."

Cambridge student Bernard Knox left a vivid account of life in the faculty: "We had smashed the huge wide windows in the American-style building (flying glass can do just as much damage as the bullets or shell-fragments that produce it) and the Madrid winter cold (which came as a surprise to Northerners like us who had been fed on tourist propaganda about sunny Spain) seeped into our bodies no matter how many blankets we wrapped around our waists. The snipers, meanwhile, made us crawl along the floor when we had to move..." The student volunteers decided to start lining up books along the window sills so that they could walk upright without giving the snipers a target. They took the thickest books they could find from the library, and Knox recalled that one was an encyclopaedia of Hindu mythology and religion. "We later discovered, after hearing bullets smack into the books, that the average penetration was to about page 350; since that discovery I am inclined to believe, as I did not before, those stories of soldiers whose lives had been saved by a Bible carried in their left-hand jacket pocket."

Knox, who was born in Bradford, survived the experience and went on to become an illustrious professor of classics at Harvard University in the United States. His heart though, he said, always remained in Spain. His friend, John Cornford, gave everything to Spain. Born into a family of distinguished academics—he was Charles Darwin's great-grandson—Cornford had one of the sharpest minds of his generation. He graduated from Cambridge in the summer of 1936 with a "starred First"—the highest degree possible. Like others of his generation, Cornford was shaken by the economic crisis of the 1930s and the rise of fascism. He became a committed communist and joined the Spanish Republican forces in August 1936. Cornford was holed up in the Faculty of Philosophy and Letters—the same library that had been established by Juana Capdevielle—when he was knocked unconscious by an exploding shell. He recovered that day, but the head wound led indirectly to his death a few weeks later. At the beginning of December, Cornford insisted on joining the newly formed British Battalion of the International Brigades and was sent to the Andalucia front in the south of Spain. Still recovering from the injury sustained in the university library, Cornford's head was covered in a large white bandage. It made him a conspicuous target. On 27 December 1936—his 21st birthday—he was killed in a charge on rebel lines, although quite what happened has never been established and his body was never recovered.

Exhaustion finally overtook both armies in the final days of November 1936. The intensity of the battle for the university campus gradually subsided and would never again reach the ferocious heights of the previous two weeks. By December it was evident that the battle for control of the Casa de Campo and the Ciudad Universitaria had degenerated into a war of attrition. Both sides fortified the buildings they held. Supply lines were protected with a maze of deep trenches which stretched in all directions across the university campus, the Parque del Oeste, and the Casa de Campo. Skirmishing continued in the sector until the end of the war, but with nothing like the ferocity of the fighting for those two weeks in November 1936.

The hospital continued to be a death trap, and the danger of being blown up by a mine was ever present; in the Parque del Oeste alone more than 200 underground mines were exploded during the course of the war. On other sectors of

The Faculty of Medicine (center) and Dentistry (right). The Hospital Clínico is on the hill behind. (Biblioteca Nacional de España, fondo fotográfico de la guerra civil española)

the front, however, boredom was often the most persistent enemy. Each side bombarded the other not with shells but with incessant propaganda and music broadcast over huge mobile loudspeakers. Troops engaged in a monotonous daily routine of observation duty, cleaning guns, maintaining their fortifications, and avoiding snipers. The strictly timetabled day of the Nationalist 1st Division shows that their infantry even slotted in a daily "siesta" between 2 and 3PM each afternoon.

Far away, in New York, the glitterati of American culture packed the Carnegie Hall and thundered their applause when Ernest Hemingway told them that the fascists "had been beaten in Parque del Oeste..." Extraordinarily it was true. Against the odds and all expectations, Madrid had held off the Nationalist assault. *No Pasarán* had turned out to be more than just a slogan. Exactly what the defense cost in terms of human life will never be known. Colonel Rojo said that any attempt to give precise numbers would

Soldiers enjoy a meal in the Parque del Oeste. (Google Art Project)

be "naïve" or "arbitrary" because of the "total confusion which reigned in public administration." After the precipitous exit of the government to Valencia on 8 November, those leaders who remained were too busy fighting to count the cost of defending the city. Mourning families and friends were left to do that alone.

The battle along Madrid's western front was vital for the survival of the city, and its vestiges can still be seen at many points today. Indeed, after his victory in 1939, General Franco reflected on the idea of leaving the university campus as it was on the last day of the war—wrecked buildings surrounded by trenches and dug outs—as a permanent memorial to *his* troops who had fought there. (The town of Belchite in the region of Aragon in the north of Spain has been left like this.) Instead Franco opted to build a monumental arch still known on the maps as the Arco de la Victoria (Victory Arch) and a mausoleum in Moncloa to the Nationalist troops who fell. (18) On a clear day, facing away from the mausoleum and looking through the dead center of the arch, Franco's somber, sinister, and monumental tomb built into the mountains of the *sierra* is clearly visible (see Chapter 7). Much smaller, and of course more recent, is a small memorial to the volunteers of the International Brigades, which now stands in the center of the campus square, opposite the Faculty of Medicine by the Ciudad Universitaria Metro station.

VISITING MADRID'S WESTERN FRONT

Any of the places listed below can be visited as separate sites. They are accessible on foot, by bicycle—and even by cable car. The Casa de Campo and Parque del Oeste are popular spots for walkers, joggers, and cyclists.

Bike rental is available in the center of Madrid. A cable car, known as the Teleférico, runs from Paseo del Pintor Rosales into the Casa de Campo. The entrance to the cable car is in Parque del Oeste behind the children's playground at the junction between Paseo del Pintor Rosales and the Calle Marqués de Urquijo. The views from the Teleférico are spectacular.

SUGGESTED ROUTE

For the traveler who is tight for time, I would suggest this route, which covers essential points with an approximate walking time of two and a half hours.

Start at the Parque Debod viewpoint (1) and walk along Paseo del Pintor Rosales (12). Enter Parque del Oeste (7), walk down to and then cross over the Paseo Ruperto Chapi. Then walk directly up the other side of the park. Some fifty meters before reaching the Avenida Séneca, you will see the three machine gun posts on the left, which stood on the Nationalist front line facing across the park to the Republican positions. (2)

Cross the Avenida Séneca via the crossing at the top of the park. Walk along the main road past the Casa de Brazil and cross the road by the Museo del Traje (Dress Museum). Immediately

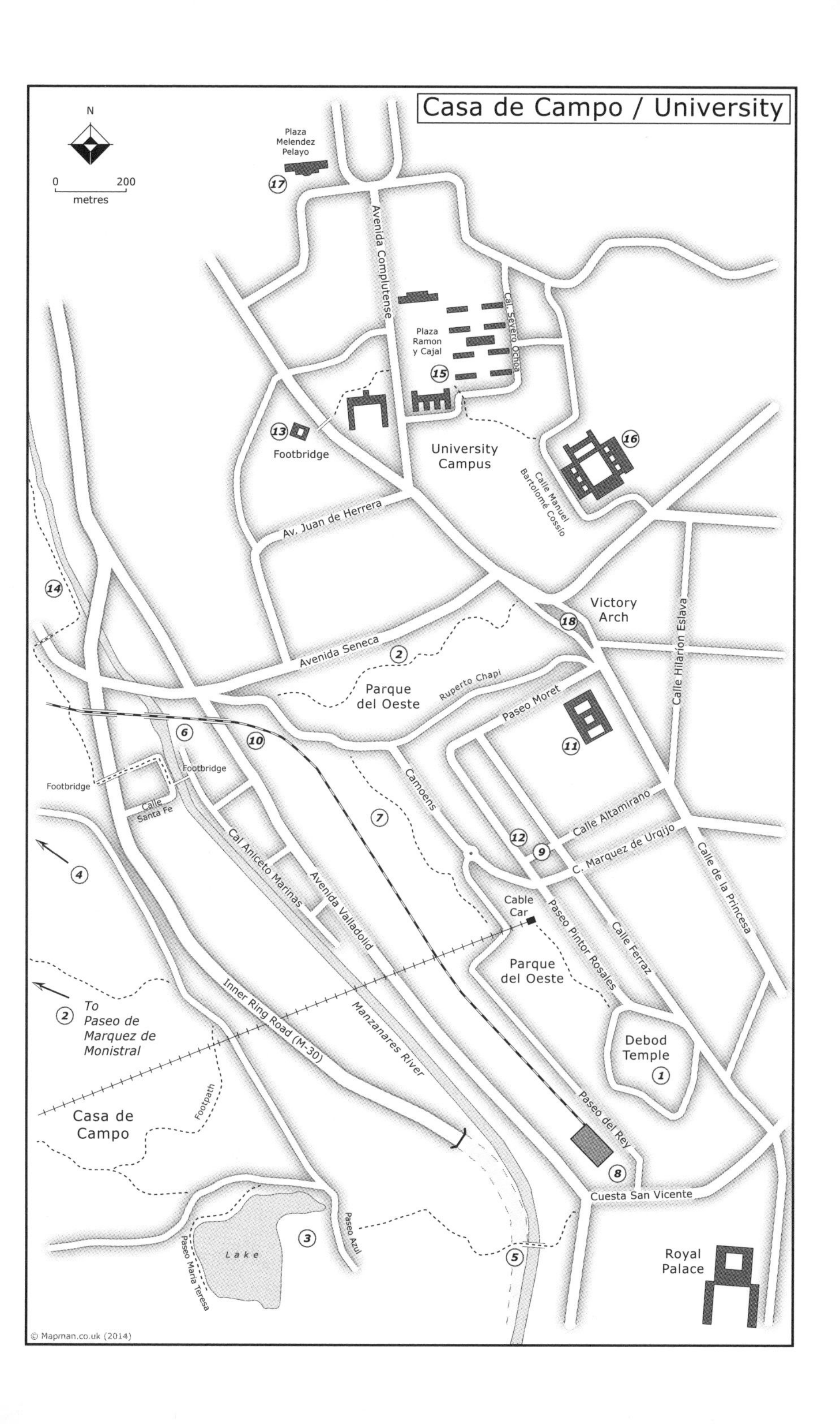

Casa de Campo / University
N
0
200
metres
Plaza Melendez Pelayo
17
Avenida Complutense
Cal. Severo Ochoa
Plaza Ramon y Cajal
15
13
Footbridge
University Campus
16
Calle Manuel Bartolomé Cossío
Av. Juan de Herrera
14
Victory Arch
18
Calle Hilarión Eslava
Avenida Seneca
2
Parque del Oeste
Ruperto Chapi
Paseo Moret
11
6
10
Footbridge
Footbridge
Calle Santa Fe
Camoens
7
Calle Altamirano
12
9
C. Marquez de Urqijo
Calle de la Princesa
4
Cal Aniceto Marinas
Avenida Valladolid
Cable Car
Paseo Pintor Rosales
Calle Ferraz
Parque del Oeste
Inner Ring Road (M-30)
Manzanares River
2
To Paseo de Marquez de Monistral
Debod Temple
1
Casa de Campo
Footpath
Paseo del Rey
8
Cuesta San Vicente
Lake
3
Paseo Azul
Paseo Maria Teresa
5
Royal Palace
© Mapman.co.uk (2014)

behind the museum is the Casa Velázquez. (14) Cross over the main road via the iron footbridge and walk towards the university, keeping the large Faculty of Agriculture to the right hand side. After 100 meters, this path leads to Plaza Ramón y Cajal, the main square of the university. The memorial to the International Brigades is on a grass bank on the left hand side. The Faculty of Philosophy, where Cornford fought, is a ten-minute walk along the Avenida Complutense, the main road running through the square. (17)

Return to the main square. The Faculty of Medicine is across the square behind the Metro station Ciudad Universitaria. The Faculty of Medicine has three wings which extend into the square. The left hand side of each wing is peppered with bullet and shrapnel holes—the fighting came from this direction. (15)

Turn right and walk on, keeping the Faculty of Medicine on your left. The steps through the pine trees lead up to the Hospital Clínico, scene of the most vicious fighting for the university campus. (16) The deep mine craters are at the top of the hill on the left.

Walk down past the hospital to the Museo de América and along the footpath past the Victory Arch. (18) Across the road is the Ministerio del Aire (Air Ministry). This building occupies the site of the old Model Prison. (11)

You are also at the Moncloa interchange, where the regular Metro and buses connect with many other parts of the city.

ROUTE NOTES

(1) The view behind the Egyptian Templo Debod looks out westwards over the Casa de Campo. The Royal Palace can be seen on the left. The main road from Madrid to the west of the Iberian Peninsula is clearly discernible. To the north of the road (on the right hand side) is the wooded Casa de Campo, through which General Franco's troops arrived when they laid siege to the city in November 1936. South of the highway (on the left hand side) is urbanized. Although considerably built up in recent

Remains of a machine gun post in the Parque del Oeste by Avenida Séneca. (James Ferguson)

years, these were traditional working-class areas which, even in the 1930s, were exactly the districts which Franco wanted to avoid fighting through while advancing on Madrid.

(2) In the Casa de Campo, some of the best preserved machine gun posts and trenches can be found 500 meters up the Paseo Marqués de Monistrol on the right-hand side. More accessible machine gun posts also remain in the Parque del Oeste by the Avenida Séneca. On a pathway just off this main road are three large machine gun posts, then known as the Holy Trinity by Nationalist troops. They were constructed in 1937 and are on what was then the Nationalist frontline. The Republican defense faced them across the other side of the park with a "no man's land" of around 250 meters between them.

(3) The lake is by Paseo Azul at the entry to the park from the Puente del Rey (King's Bridge). The ground between Paseo Azul and Paseo María Teresa is clearly churned up from the war.

(4) The Cerro Garabitas is visible from many parts of the Casa de Campo and easily identifiable today because of an observation platform at its top, which is used by the city fire service. The entrance to the cable car is in Parque del Oeste behind the children's playground at the junction between Paseo del Pintor Rosales and the Calle Marqués de Urquijo.

(5) The Puente del Rey leads across from the Royal Palace to a main entrance into the Casa de Campo. The River Manzanares has recently been extensively remodeled along this section.

(6) The Puente de los Franceses looks today almost exactly as it did in November 1936. The river was wider then and has since been canalized. The best view is from the small footbridge

The Puente de los Franceses across the Manzanares river (Martius/Wikimedia Commons)

about 100 meters downriver between Calle Aniceto Marinas and Calle Santa Fe. The lower road bridge called Puente Nuevo can be seen next to the Puente de los Franceses.

(7) Parque del Oeste (West Park) was opened in 1901 and landscaped to create an "English-style garden" on the western side of Madrid. Trenches and gun emplacements were built throughout the park during the Civil War and there was extensive mining activity. It was estimated that over 200 explosions took place *underneath* the park in addition to the thousands of shells which were fired over it. The park was extensively replanted after the war, but some of the statues bear testimony to the fighting: the monument to Dr. Federico Rubio in the center of the park is still there, scarred by the battle. And even now debris can appear. Early in 2013, the author's wife discovered a bullet fired into the park during the war.

(8) The Estación del Norte yard is on the corner of Cuesta San Vicente and Paseo del Rey. The station is now called Principe Pío. A melancholy air hangs around the abandoned yard and old booking offices of the Estación del Norte. It is not difficult to imagine the volunteers of the International Brigades as they mustered here on 8 November before going over the river to fight in the Casa de Campo. In 1941 the station hosted the arrival of Nazi leader Heinrich Himmler on what the Franco regime treated as a state visit. Other parts of the station, however, have been renovated as a commercial and cinema complex.

(9) One of the small streets which run up from Paseo del Pintor Rosales and the Parque del Oeste is the Calle Altamirano. The lively neighborhood bar Casa Paco (34 Calle Altamirano) has an old sepia photograph of the barricaded street as it was during the war. The bar is also a good spot to stop for a cheap drink and serving of *tortilla.* At the top of the Calle Altamirano is an apartment block known as the Casa de las Flores (on the corner of Calle Princesa and Calle Hilarión Eslava). The Chilean poet

The Casa de las Flores and barricades on the corner of Calle Princesa and Calle Hilarión Eslava (Biblioteca Nacional de España, fondo fotográfico de la guerra civil española)

and diplomat Pablo Neruda lived here until his flat was shelled in November 1936. The photograph shows the Casa de las Flores and barricaded street.

(10) The ferocity of the fighting can be gauged by looking at the brick-built Casa del Jardinero (Gardener's Hut) near the Puente de los Franceses. The one-story building is on Avenida Valladolid just before the railway bridge opposite the Hospital Clínica Moncloa. The north and western sides of the building which faced the Nationalist onslaught are still peppered with the marks from bullets and shrapnel.

(11) The Cárcel Modelo (Model Prison), inaugurated in 1883, was based on designs by the British utilitarian thinker Jeremy Bentham. It was right on the Republican front line during the war and virtually destroyed by the fighting. The Ministerio del Aire (air ministry), built on the foundations of the old prison, stands on the site today.

(12) Paseo del Pintor Rosales runs along the Parque del Oeste. It was—and is—one of the smartest streets in Madrid; politicians, diplomats, and film stars are among its exclusive residents. When writers Ernest Hemingway, John Dos Passos, and Dutch filmmaker Joris Ivens made a documentary film about the Spanish Civil War called *The Spanish Earth*, they based themselves in a bombed out apartment on Paseo del Pintor Rosales (Hemingway called it the "Old Homestead"). From this vantage point they recorded some of best footage of fighting in the Casa de Campo, park, and university city. The film can be seen on YouTube: http://www.youtube.com/watch?v=MT8q6VAyTi8

(13) The Casa Velázquez is now owned by a French foundation and access to the building is only possible with prior permission. The Faculty of Architecture is 100 meters downhill from Casa Velázquez.

(14) The *pasarela de la muerte* was about 500 meters north (upstream from the Puente de los Franceses). The spot can still be seen today and is easily accessible—the route along the Manzaneres is popular with cyclists, joggers, and walkers. Start at the small footbridge across the Manzanares between Calle Aniceto Marinas and Calle Santa Fe (about 100 meters downriver from the Puente de los Franceses). Walk 150 meters up the Calle Santa Fe to a foot/bike bridge which leads into the Casa de Campo. Cross over the bridge. On the other side of the bridge, turn right along the pedestrianized road (marked on maps as Puente de Castilla) for some 200 meters. Cross under the railway bridge. Immediately beyond the railway bridge, to the right, is a footpath/cycle path which leads over the large, single-span bridge. Cross the bridge,

which leads back down to the Manzanares river. The foot/cycle path now leads between the river on the right hand side and the Sabatini brick wall on the left. About 200 meters along the track there are different colors of brick work. This was the location of the *pasarela de la muerte.* The place is marked with a sign and photograph of the bridge erected by a local history group, although this is sometimes vandalized.

(15) The Complutense university Faculties of Medicina (Medicine), Farmacia (Pharmacy), and Odontología (Orthodontics) are on three sides of the Plaza Ramón y Cajal. This is the main *plaza,* or square, of the university. The entrance to the Metro station Ciudad Universitaria (University City) is in the square. The bullet and shrapnel marks can best be seen on the right hand wings of the Faculty of Medicine which is directly behind the Metro station entrance. The small memorial to the International Brigades is across the Avenida Complutense, directly in front of the Metro station.

(16) The Hospital Clínico is on the Calle de Manuel Bartolomé Cossio. The hospital was extensively rebuilt after the war, although the original sections can be identified because the bricks are of a different color. The hospital is at the top of a steep slope which rises from behind the Faculties of Medicine and Orthodontics on the university campus. At top of this slope and adjacent to the hospital, two massive craters left by the mines are still clearly visible.

(17) The Faculty of Philosophy and Letters is in the Plaza Menéndez Pelayo on the university campus. The building was badly damaged in the conflict but rebuilt exactly according to the original design. It was reopened on 13 October 1943—the Spanish national day—and a plaque in the main foyer proudly records that "El Generalísimo Francisco Franco" presided over the ceremony. Above the main entrance to the building a (now faded) inscription in Latin commands the visitor to remember those who died fighting for the building. The list carved into the portal is also worn now, but records the names of fallen

Nationalist soldiers. Of the library staff like Juana Capdevielle, or the volunteers like John Cornford, there is no mention anywhere in the building. But the library is still there and can be reached by walking along the corridor on the right-hand side of the entrance hall. The friendly library staff may allow visitors in to look around (if the reading room is not too busy) and show them books about the university during the war.

(18) The Arch is an unavoidable landmark in the district. Some 60 meters tall, it looms over the edge of the university campus and the middle of the main road into Madrid from the northwest.

The Arco de la Victoria build by Franco to celebrate the crushing of one half of Spain by the other half. (David Mathieson)

6

THE BATTLE OF JARAMA: GENERAL FRANCO'S PLAN C

"Death stalked the olive trees
Picking his men
His leadened finger beckoned
Again and again"

John Lepper, volunteer with the British Battalion of the XV International Brigade and survivor of the Battle of Jarama

In the early hours of the morning on 12 February 1937 a fleet of lorries pulled up outside a farmhouse in the Jarama Valley some 30 kilometers southeast of Madrid. About 500 British lads jumped out, pulling their rucksacks after them, and headed into the courtyard of the house, where they were given hot black coffee and bread. One of them later recalled that they looked to all the world like a group about to go on a Sunday outing. But this was to be no picnic. In less than 72 hours, more than half the group would be dead or badly wounded. For the rest, none of their lives would ever be the same again.

The Battle of Jarama was one of the most important actions in the entire Civil War. Frustrated in their attempts to take Madrid from the west, General Franco's Nationalist forces launched a massive onslaught to the southeast of the city. The objective was to cut off the main road between Madrid and Valencia. The highway was the capital's umbilical cord—vital supplies of food, fuel, and munitions passed along the road to the besieged capital. The Nationalist offensive was halted only in the nick of time and had it not been for the intervention of the International Brigades, Madrid would undoubtedly have fallen. The volunteers were in the vanguard of the forces which struggled to stem the Nationalist advance and suffered heavy losses. Today the valley is an idyllic rural landscape, the hills covered by olive groves and wild herbs. Yet amidst the quiet, the remains of battle are still very much in evidence, a silent testament to the volunteers' astonishing courage.

The uprising of 18 July 1936 was intended as a swift military *coup* to overthrow the Republican government. This was the rebels' plan A, and it failed. The troops at the Montaña Barracks did not join the revolt (see Chapter 4), and General Mola's army was unable to break through the Sierra de Guadarrama (see Chapter 7). General Franco's Army of Africa then marched on Madrid, but was unable to breach the defense on the western side of the city (see Chapter 5). This signaled the failure of the rebels' plan B. Yet the city remained the prize which would determine the outcome of the war—despite the Republican government's flight to Valencia in early November 1936, Madrid continued to be recognized as the strategic key to control of the country.

Over Christmas 1936 Nationalist commanders began to formulate their plan C, a new offensive to the south of Madrid. To break the impasse, Franco decided on a maneuver which would circumvent Madrid from the south and cut across the road to Valencia. The Mediterranean sea port was not only now the seat of government, but a vital gateway for supplies of food and raw materials. With the link broken, Madrid would be effectively besieged on three sides. A successful attack would rupture effective communication with the government and leave the city in an untenable position.

Franco's new offensive was planned for January 1937. Nationalist troops were moved from the Casa de Campo, west of Madrid, to points along the line in the southeast of the city. The offensive was delayed for a couple of weeks by appalling winter weather, but on 6 February they moved out from various points along the valley of the River Jarama. (The valley is on the eastern side of Madrid and runs from north to south.) It was a massive assault involving some 25,000 ground troops.

It was also a battle for control of the skies where the Italian Fiats and German Heinkels on the Nationalist side fought it out with Russian Polikarpovs for the Republicans. Colonel Vicente Rojo, the able second in command of the defense of Madrid, later wrote that "the first great air battle in the history of warfare was unleashed over the skies of Jarama." In that sense, Jarama was an important transitional battle on the road to modern warfare. Both sides struggled for superiority in the air while cavalry charged—for one of the last times in thousands of years of war—on the ground.

General Enríque Varela (who had organized the assault on Madrid before Christmas) was once again the Nationalist field commander. The initial phase of the attack caught the Republicans by surprise and was a considerable success. That sector of the front was poorly defended—partly because of squabbling between two Republican commanders, Generals Miaja and Pozas. General Miaja was responsible for the defense of Madrid and held firm to the erroneous belief that the Nationalists would attack the south of the city, where he was cautiously prepared. General Pozas, commander of the Republican Army of the Center, correctly calculated the point of the next Nationalist offensive and pleaded for reinforcements to buttress defenses along the Valencia road. He was rebuffed by Miaja, however, who refused to redeploy "his" troops from Madrid to protect the highway.

While the two commanders bickered, the Nationalists quickly overran the Republicans' forward defensive positions.

Intelligence and communications were poor, and the Republicans had only a hazy idea of the forces ranged against them. Republican Colonel Rojo confessed that the early reports which reached Madrid about the offensive were "late, of poor quality, and came mainly through prisoners taken." These intelligence failures and lack of coordination would have fateful consequences for the British volunteers of the XV International Brigade. Meanwhile, the rebels were making important gains and driving the Republican forces back towards the east. By 9 February, Nationalist morale was riding high; Franco himself arrived at the headquarters of the commanding officer to witness the next phase of the offensive, which would be to cross the Jarama river.

On the evening of 10 February, French and Belgian volunteers from the International Brigade arranged their sentry duty at one of the river crossings, called the Puente Pindoque (Pindoque Bridge). The volunteers, who had arrived just a few hours before, set up machine guns at either end of the bridge but had little more time to reconnoiter the surrounding area or properly orientate themselves in their unfamiliar surroundings. Without hot food—fire and smoke gave away positions—they prepared for a long, cold night. Most did not live to see the dawn. In the early hours of the morning a company of Moroccan soldiers slipped across the river and slit the guards' throats. They then cut the wires to the detonators and began to hurl grenades into the encampment of the stunned volunteers.

Hundreds of Nationalist troops—with cavalry, artillery, and supplies—now crossed over the river and prepared to continue the offensive. The breach in the Republican line grew wider as the day wore on. By evening, more Republican forces had been pushed back from the river bank and the Nationalists were able to take the next bridge downriver to the south, by the small town of San Martín de la Vega.

On 12 February, a formidable section of the Nationalist army had crossed the river and was now on the eastern bank. But the

British volunteers who rolled up outside the farmhouse before dawn knew nothing of this. The limited intelligence available suggested that most of the Nationalist forces were still on the western side of the Jarama Valley. It was not understood that a large number had now crossed the river. As far as the volunteers were aware, their task would be to reinforce the Republican defenses along the eastern banks of the River Jarama several kilometers away down in the valley. It was a fatal miscalculation.

While the Nationalists advanced up the Jarama Valley, the British Battalion had been pulled out of their base in Madrigueras, a small town on the road to Valencia some 200 kilometers from Madrid. They moved out on 11 February. After a long, uncomfortable journey by rail and road, the men arrived in the evening at the medieval village of Chinchón, just 15 kilometers from the Jarama Valley. For most of them this was to be their first time in action: they slept little, listening to the artillery barrage somewhere to the west. In the early hours of the morning they were loaded onto trucks again and driven the final leg of their journey to muster at a remote farmhouse—which rapidly became known as the Cookhouse—on the edge of the valley. (1) By the time they arrived there at 5AM on 12 February most were already exhausted by the long journey and sleepless night. They were cheered slightly by the bulky battalion chef known as "Tiny" Silverman who dispensed their breakfast of bread and coffee.

The men explored the building, which had been the country retreat of a renowned cartoonist called Borgaria. His irreverent work was well-known and published in the *El Sol* newspaper. This liberal daily had been founded in 1917 to provide a platform for just the kind of moderate, progressive, middle-class opinion-formers whose voices were being drowned out by the Civil War. Over the years Borgaria had been arrested, beaten, and harassed for mocking those with power but his wit remained undimmed. Iconoclastic cartoons lampooning the Spanish ruling elite (especially the clergy) decorated many walls and delighted the volunteers. One of Spain's pin-up bullfighters and a cultural icon, Ignacio Sánchez Mejías, had been such a regular guest in the house that he had his own bedroom there. Mejías moved from fame to immortality in 1934 when he was gored to death in the bullring, an event described by the poet Federico García Lorca in one of his best poems, "A las cinco de la tarde" (At Five in the Afternoon).

Some of the men milled around outside the Cookhouse trying to orientate themselves and speculating on enemy positions. In the dark the silhouettes of the undulating hills and regular olive groves look disarmingly similar—and the landscape became even more confusing to volunteers as the day wore on. The nearest town, Morata de Tajuña, some five kilometers away in the valley of the Tajuña river, emerged into view as the sun rose to burn off the morning mist. (2)

The commander of the British Battalion at Jarama was Captain Tom Wintringham, a product of the private Gresham's School and Balliol College, Oxford. Slightly stooped and bookish in appearance, he reminded some other volunteers of a school teacher. Wintringham came from a comfortable middle-class and highly political family (both his uncle and, unusually, his aunt had been Liberal MPs). Following active service in World War I, Wintringham went into journalism and then the law. But it was politics which provided his mainspring: he joined the Communist Party in the 1920s, and went to Spain soon after the outbreak of the war, in August 1936.

Wintringham took some scouts and set off west toward the front and the sound of gunfire on a reconnaissance mission. Behind the Cookhouse the ground rises steeply to a plateau. The raised ground extends some three kilometers west until it begins to fall away again to the valley floor of the Jarama river. The plateau is known as the Cerro Pingarrón and rises up from the valley floor—although after the battle the British gave the heights a new name: Suicide Hill.

Wintringham and his group made their way west along the

highway which leads from Morata to San Martín de la Vega. They then turned down the Cañada Galiana—a track used since time immemorial as a right of way for locals with their oxcarts and livestock. The traffic of centuries has eroded the pathway to a depth of around a meter into the surrounding fields and olive groves—so the British called it the "sunken road." (3) Over the next three days this track became a central reference point in the chaos of the battle. It is still there today and follows exactly the same course, although in parts it is now a little wider and shallower. The view of the Jarama Valley from the sunken road is spectacular. Among the quiet of the olive groves the air is also perfumed by the pungent aroma of the wild flowers and herbs like rosemary, thyme, marjoram, and oregano. It is not difficult to imagine the scene which the British volunteers encountered 80 years ago, and today the position is marked with a small memorial. (4)

Standing on the western ridge of the plateau, the group gazed across the valley to survey what they thought was the frontline down by the river. Beyond they could see the city of Madrid and, in the distance, the snow-capped peaks of the Guadarrama mountain range. One of Wintringham's scouts, the 27-year-old sculptor Jason Gurney, was unhurriedly sketching maps of the area. Gurney was impressed by the beauty of the panoramic views in the early spring sunshine. He described the scene as idyllic and the reconnaissance mission as "rather like a school field day." From the valley below, however, came the clearly audible rumble of artillery fire and the occasional stray shot even reached the plateau. As they were observing the scene, one of the British party was hit in the arm. Gurney was more irritated than scared and felt that it was "vaguely unsporting" that a shot from an "anonymous soldier miles away" should interrupt the group's deliberations.

The British continued to take their bearings and rendezvoused with the commander of the XV International Brigade, János Gálicz, who was also taking stock of the positions. Gálicz, better

The ancient cattle trail worn away by centuries of use and known to the British as the "sunken road." The battle raged through the olive groves on either side. (James Ferguson)

known to the volunteers as "General Gal," was a Hungarian who had been captured by the Russians in World War I. He became a communist during the Bolshevik Revolution of 1917 and underwent training at Moscow's famous Frunze Military Academy. Aloof and somewhat mysterious—it was said that he spoke German with a Slavic accent and Russian with a German accent—Gal was not popular with the volunteers who generally thought him cold and arrogant. The next few days revealed worse deficiencies: an incompetence verging on the callous. Ernest Hemingway said that Gal "should have been shot" for some of the orders he gave at Jarama. In the end he was indeed shot, though quite why remains unclear. Stalin ordered Gal's return to Moscow in 1939, and there he was executed in the dictator's Great Purge.

Gal explained that the Franco-Belgian Battalion was positioned immediately to the north of the Morata-San Martín de la Vega road. The British were to take up positions south of the road. He then scrawled lines in blue pencil on a crude map of the area which pointed due west towards the Nationalist positions down in the valley. "Your men will advance at once in this direction," he told Wintringham before turning on his heel and leaving the British party. The English captain hurried back down the Morata road to his men in the Cookhouse. After the officers were briefed the men were mustered and at 10AM the volunteers of the British Battalion moved out to follow Gal's orders.

The battalion was split into four companies. Nos. 1, 3, and 4 were infantry companies armed with rifles and a few light automatic machine guns, while no. 2 was the heavy machine gun company armed with eight Maxim guns. They left the Cookhouse behind them heading due west cross country over ground heavy with the recent torrential rain. But the morning was clear and the temperature soon began to rise in the bright spring sunshine. The men sweated their way up the steep embankment onto the plateau, discarding whatever they could to lighten their load. One recalled later that the hillside looked like an "abandoned fairground" littered with excrement and magazines of all kinds from copies of the *Daily Worker* to third-rate pornography. The discarded books included Shakespeare, innumerable volumes of poetry, Spanish phrasebooks, and, predictably, a range of political tomes from *Mein Kampf* to *Das Kapital.* More alarmingly, men also started to discard heavy overcoats and blankets and left them neatly stowed under trees. Did they think that they would be returning to the Cookhouse at the end of the day? One company officer with military experience knew better. He berated the volunteers and urged them not to abandon anything that would keep them warm at night on the exposed plateau.

The men of the Machine Gun Company set off last and had the most difficult task. The eight Maxim guns they carried were undoubtedly still effective and could discharge 500 rounds a minute to a range of up to a kilometer. But they were antiquated pieces from World War I and heavy—each weighed 140lb. Even broken up into their component parts they were cumbersome to lug over the Spanish countryside. The company's 70 men were soon exhausted. Much more serious was an error discovered soon after the company moved off: they had been supplied with the wrong ammunition. Company Commander Lieutenant Harry Fry, an Edinburgh cobbler who had served as an army sergeant in World War I, quickly spotted the mistake and immediately dispatched men to locate cartridges of the correct caliber. The right ammunition eventually arrived later in the day—but only after a delay which cost the battalion dear.

By late morning the infantrymen of 1, 3, and 4 Companies reached the sunken road where Wintringham had rendezvoused with Gal earlier in the day. They had little idea of the enemy position but followed Gal's orders and began to advance west. The companies broke up into smaller units and fanned out to cover a stretch of nearly two kilometers south of the Morata-San Martín road. One inexperienced volunteer was soon surprised by what he thought were large numbers of noisy crickets in the area, while another noted that there were an unusual number of birds whistling. The noises were caused not by innocuous wildlife, however, but live ammunition.

The rebels were in fact much closer to the British position than anyone had anticipated, and events now began to move quickly. In less than an hour the British understanding of what they were expected to do was swept away by a new and lethal reality. The volunteers believed that they were being asked to reinforce Republican positions down in the valley. In fact, they were walking into a firestorm. Having crossed the River Jarama, some 2,000 crack rebel troops were less than a couple of kilometers away and were heading straight for the British Battalion.

For every one British volunteer on the hillside of the Jarama Valley that day there were at least three seasoned Nationalist soldiers, mainly from the Army of Africa and the Spanish

The remains of the British Battalion at Jarama. Fred Copeman is standing sixth from the left. (Marx Memorial Library, London)

Foreign Legion. These elite infantrymen carried modern rifles, hand grenades, and machetes. They were supported by a company from the German Condor Legion armed with eight heavy machine guns and four mortars. It was a formidable force which would have tested army professionals, let alone raw volunteers. Yet the British Battalion was all that stood between the rebels and the Valencia road.

The 600 volunteers clustered in small groups and spread across the hillocks were rapidly engulfed by the Nationalist onslaught. "It hit us before you knew what was happening," recalled a survivor, John "Bosco" Jones. Volunteer Patrick Curry said the fire increased with the enemy advancing rapidly like "little specks" towards him. Suddenly all the manifold deficiencies of their weaponry, training, and communications became mercilessly apparent. The most immediate concern was with the weapons. The Nationalist troops were armed with German Mausers, renowned for their accuracy and reliability. The weapons carried by the volunteers were not. Models of various makes and ages had been supplied to the battalion so that the men required five different types of ammunition simply to keep firing in unison. The Colts and French "shosser" light automatic weapons were the worst, both jamming with alarming frequency. Bosco Jones described them as "fucking useless... just fucking useless" and they were discarded within an hour.

Others now began to rue the lack of weapons training at Madrigueras, the base where the men had been held on stand-by during the previous weeks. Brigadier Albert Charlesworth said that when the action began at Jarama, "it was the very first time I had ever fired a rifle in my life," and many men did not even initially realize that their rifle sights needed to be set according to the distance from the target. This meant that the bullet struck the ground way short even if the line was true. Jason Gurney reflected that "no one in Madrigueras had said anything about artillery fire or the genius of Moorish infantry to move across country without presenting a target for anyone but a highly trained marksman—a category that included no one in our outfit."

The battalion was also hampered by the break down in communications. Neither the Battalion HQ nor the Brigade HQ understood the sheer force of the Nationalist onslaught which hit the British volunteers. The British Battalion commander, Wintringham, had set up his HQ along the sunken road. (5) Soon, however, the commander lost sight of many of his men as they advanced on the far side of the hills in front of him, and was in no position to direct either tactics or strategy. By the time some of Wintringham's hand-scrawled instructions actually reached the front, the company commanders to whom they were addressed were already dead. Replies were equally useless because the runners took hours to return and by then the situation had changed again.

Well behind the line, the Brigade HQ understood even less. (6) While the British were being pummeled on one side of the Morata road, the Franco-Belgian Battalion was also under fierce assault on the other side. But there was no point at which any commander in the Brigade HQ could observe the front now under attack. Consequently, their decisions were based wholly on reports coming from along the front in four different languages and the delay in transmitting information meant that there were long time lags. Charles Bloom, a Jewish Cockney commercial traveler, for example, became brigade runner and interlocutor with the French further up the line. The French commander spoke no English but did speak some German. Bloom's German was better than his French so the two spoke in German which Bloom then translated back into English for the benefit of battalion staff who spoke neither French nor German. Wintringham had been issued with a field telephone to connect him with the Brigade HQ, but the line was of exceptionally poor quality, a problem compounded by the noise of battle. The fuzzy connection garbled attempts at conversation in different languages to an incomprehensible babble. And in any event, no one had any detailed maps, so trying to describe what was going on without grid references was pointless.

Despite his partial view of events, it rapidly became evident to Wintringham that his men were suddenly and unexpectedly in serious jeopardy. They urgently needed to adopt a defensive strategy and attempt to hold the line as best they could to stop the Nationalists breaking through. Yet even this would have been problematic because, without clear instructions about what was expected from them, the British had left most of their few entrenching tools back at the Cookhouse. Under increasingly heavy fire, the men were using their bayonets and helmets to try and dig in on the open hillsides. Wintringham frantically tried to inform the Brigade HQ but Gal refused to accept what he was being told. When the order came through from Brigade HQ it was not to consolidate and defend but to advance. Under the circumstances the order was simply absurd as, far from advancing, the battalion could not even hold the Nationalist surge. By mid-afternoon the volunteers were fighting with astonishing courage but were being pushed steadily back.

No. 3 Company was commanded by Lieutenant Bill Briskey, a London bus driver and veteran of World War I. Briskey had led his unit about two kilometers south down the sunken road. (4iii) They were positioned on the battalion's far left flank and came under direct and sustained heavy artillery fire. The Spanish Republican unit which was supposed to have been covering their left flank to the south was nowhere to be seen. On the other hand, the rebel Moroccan troops *were* visible to the south and edging closer; no. 3 Company was thus in imminent danger of being outflanked and cut off by a Nationalist pincer movement. Briskey started pulling his men back towards the sunken road and was killed in the retreat by a burst of machine gun fire which tore into his stomach.

Two volunteers, Christopher Caudwell and Clem Beckett, attempted to give their comrades covering fire with an old machine gun. Before the war both men had achieved fame in their own completely separate spheres. Caudwell (whose real name was St. John Sprigg) was an innovative engineer but best known as a prolific Marxist novelist, academic critic, and poet. Becket, from Oldham, was a blacksmith turned motorcycle speedway champion and stunt rider—his speciality was to jump through a flaming "wall of death." The two had forged a close, if unlikely, friendship in the Brigade. As with many other volunteers, 12 February 1937 was to be their first and last day of war: their machine gun jammed and they were overrun by Moroccans who killed them both with bayonets and machetes. By this time the battalion commander, Wintringham, had lost contact with no. 3 Company "for several hours" and sent Jason Gurney off down the sunken road to find what was happening. When Gurney reached the men he found a scene that was "really horrible. Briskey was dead and No. 3 Company had lost more than half of its total strength, either dead or wounded."

No. 4 Company was positioned on a hillock, White House Hill, 500 meters to the north of no. 3 Company. (4iv) The white farmhouse on top of the hill was a notable landmark as one of the few buildings in the area (the building was destroyed in the war and only the remains, which are on private land, can be seen today). From the hill, the men could see the rebel infantry advancing toward them through the gullies in the hillocks below. The Moroccan troops wore cloaks with a bright red lining, which made for an impressive, if unwelcome, sight. The professional soldiers made skilled use of the available cover—clefts in the rocks, trees, and bushes—and let lose a hail of fire. The exposed British positions did not stand a chance—"'we were really slashed about," in the words of one of the few survivors.

The volunteers who had advanced down the slopes beyond the White House retreated rapidly to the building and surrounding courtyard. There they huddled together for safety, apparently unaware that the conspicuous building was an ideal range finder for Nationalist artillery. After a couple of salvos to perfect sightings, a barrage of shells began to rain down on the building and those in the yard. Through the smoke chunks of masonry, clods of earth and body parts were flung high into the air from the hilltop. The remainder of the battalion looked on in horror while the men of no. 4 Company scrambled down from the hill as best they could to escape the carnage.

Firm leadership might have improved the position but the commander of no. 4 Company, Lieutenant Bert Overton, simply vanished at crucial moments during the afternoon and left his men to fend for themselves. Overton had been given command of no. 4 Company on the basis of peacetime experience in the Welsh Guards. This turned out to be a mistake. He "looked the part" and had apparently been a "brilliant" soldier on the parade ground but in the heat of the battle he simply cracked up, probably from shell-shock. Overton was seen by various eye-witnesses sheltering in fox holes and then eventually scampering toward the safety of the sunken road. The consequences of Overton's recurring erratic behavior would be calamitous for the entire battalion the following day.

No. 1 Company occupied the ground on the far right of the British line. (4i) The company was spread out about 500 meters north of the White House Hill on the next hillock, called Conical Hill (so called because from the valley floor it looks like a cone). The most immediate problem for no. 1 Company was an isolated hillock about 500 meters to the right called The Knoll. At the start of the day, when the British began to advance, it had been held by French volunteers—but not any more. The French, like the British, had taken heavy casualties and had been pushed off the hill by the Nationalist thrust. As a consequence, no. 1 Company's right flank was no longer covered by the French but wholly exposed to the Nationalists. The rebels installed a heavy machine on top of The Knoll which began to strafe the men, and now Tom Wintringham in the Battalion HQ had a clear view of what was happening:

> Machine rifles clacked and chattered from this hill [The Knoll] enfilading the [British] line. They could fire along the ranks of the three companies. They could fire into the very few small groups of men, sheltered by the hill crest from frontal fire... Their fire cut across the path to the rear down which the wounded crawled. The men who were holding the ridge could hear no sound which meant help from behind them.

One World War I veteran described the crossfire which trapped the battalion on the hillocks that afternoon as being more deadly than that of the Somme. The Irish commander of No. 1 Company, Kit Conway, tried to rally his men. Conway was an orphan and had spent his childhood in a Tipperary poorhouse. Graced with an easy charm and quick intelligence, the self-educated Conway became involved in Irish Republican guerrilla campaigns in the 1920s—all of which provided vital military experience when he arrived in Spain in the autumn of 1936. An Irish volunteer Jim Prendergast described what happened to Conway and no. 1 Company during the afternoon: "We had just swung through the bottle-neck of a valley and were beginning to deploy when we came under direct fire. Men were hurriedly seeking good cover among the scrub, but once we lay down we had no view ahead. Kit saw this at once and roared out the order to fire from standing positions."

The Company turned its fire on Nationalist troops about 400 meters to the left and was soon caught in the crossfire: "... the Fascist fire, front and flank, was now pretty heavy. Men were being hit all around. Somebody was hit beside me. A yell for stretcher bearers..." Under heavy fire, Conway ordered his men to pull back up the hill:

> Kit is standing on top of the hill. He is using a rifle himself, and after every shot turns towards the men to give instructions. Suddenly, he shouts, his rifle spins out

> of his hand, and he falls back. My God, Kit is hit in the groin. He is placed on a blanket. No stretchers left now. His voice is broken with agony. "Boys, don't leave me for the Fascists."

Conway died soon afterwards, and by late afternoon about a third of no. 1 Company's men were dead too. The remainder huddled on the south side of the hill wondering how they could retreat without being killed. To the north, the Franco-Belgian Battalion had collapsed and had been pushed way back past the British position. The Spanish Battalion which had been promised to fight alongside the British to the south simply never materialized. A renewed Nationalist thrust from either flank would leave hundreds of men on the ridge trapped. Isolated in a pincer movement, they would be taken prisoner—if they were lucky.

By late afternoon it was clear that the battalion could not hold the ridge for much longer. Wintringham sent orders for the men to pull back to the relative cover of the sunken road, although some had already fled and others were caught in a deadly crossfire as they picked their way through the olive groves. Maurice Davidovitch, a young Jewish Londoner and commander of the stretcher bearers who had worked tirelessly all afternoon to bring the wounded back from the ridge, was one. His comrade Fred Copeman saw what happened next. "A burst of machine-rifle fire ripped out his stomach… his guts fell out but he just picked them up in his hands and stuffed them all back again with blood running down his legs." Despite his protestations to leave him, Davidovitch's comrades pulled him back to the sunken road.

As the evening sun set behind Madrid and the Guadarrama mountain range in the west, the fading light seemed to signal the demise of the British resistance too. The volunteers had been pummeled for hours in an unequal struggle on the hillsides, and though they had put up an incredibly brave fight, the battalion was now broken and concerned only with covering its retreat. The Nationalist commanders' thoughts turned to sweeping the ridge of remaining stragglers and pushing on. Cleared of British resistance, the way was open to take the Valencia road beyond and, inexorably, defeat the Republic.

These were all reasonable assumptions—and they were all wrong. It had been a frustrating day for Lieutenant Harry Fry and the machine gunners of no. 2 Company under his command. Despite having been supplied with the wrong ammunition, the men had nevertheless lugged the guns to the front and set up the old Maxims in a forward position on the heights overlooking the valley. (4ii) But until the correct ammunition arrived they could not fire a shot. Their impotence was matched by the anger of those in the other companies who were being mauled on the hillsides in front of them.

Fry had despatched a lorry to collect the correct cartridges from stores held in the local town of Morata as soon as he realized that a mistake had been made. There the truck was loaded with the correct ammunition and sent off to the front, but driving a truck full of ammunition into a war zone requires some nerve and the driver downed several brandies to steady himself. Drunk, he overturned his lorry on the winding road up from Morata to the plateau and then fled. The abandoned vehicle was only located during the afternoon, still some distance from the front, and the heavy boxes had to be carted by hand through the olive groves to the waiting Maxims. Only then could the gunners start the painstaking task of loading the cartridges into the belts. Later in the afternoon more vital cartridges arrived when a second ammunition truck, driven by the young Secretary of Mitcham's Labour Party branch, picked its way gingerly down the sunken road. Narrowly avoiding being shelled, the lorry took cover under the olive trees to the rear of the Maxims where it was unloaded.

No. 2 Company was now ready to join the fray, but the Moroccan troops did not know this. Fred Copeman, who took effective command of the machine guns, saw "a long line of Moorish troops with officers on horses, flowing cloaks red and blue as if they were on a bloody Sunday parade" coming up the valley. Copeman was one of the most experienced soldiers in the British unit. Born in a workhouse and separated from his family at an early age, he had joined the Royal Navy as a youth. While traveling the world he learned how to box and won money as a heavyweight prize fighter. It was political struggle, however, that consumed him. Copeman was discharged from the Navy for his part in the Invergordon Mutiny in 1931 (when, for the only time in British naval history, ratings rebelled against a pay cut) and joined the Communist Party. He was admired and feared by the other volunteers who were awed by his courage in the face of the enemy, although others resented him as a bully. At that particular moment, though, Copeman's forceful leadership was just what the company needed.

He ordered the gunners to hold fire to avoid being prematurely located by the Nationalist artillery. The more inexperienced volunteers could scarcely contain their fear as Copeman prowled up and down behind them while 300 to 400 crack Moroccan troops advanced ever closer. When one terrified volunteer looked as though he was about to break ranks and open fire, Copeman laid him out with a single punch. When the Moroccans were within 50 to 60 meters, silhouetted by the setting sun behind them, Copeman gave the order and the gunners finally opened up. As the British strafed the Nationalist lines in unison from right to left, score upon score of Moroccan infantrymen "went down like corn." The volleys continued until none of them was left alive: "one or two may have got away but I did not see them... our Battalion annihilated one of the finest units of Franco's army in a few minutes," Copeman recalled.

The terms upon which the battle was being fought had suddenly changed dramatically. Now both sides were reeling from a day of brutal combat and the costs were terrible. As dusk fell Jason Gurney went to reconnoiter the southern end of the sunken road. After about 700 meters he stumbled upon about 50 wounded men on stretchers who had simply been forgotten in the chaos of the battle and retreat: "They had appalling wounds, mostly from artillery. One little Jewish kid [possibly Davidovich] of about eighteen lay on his back with his bowels exposed from his navel to his genitals and his intestines lying in a ghastly pinkish brown heap, twitching slightly as the flies searched over them. He was perfectly conscious..." Another man had nine bullet holes across his chest. Gurney talked to him for a while and held his hand until death overtook him and it went limp. "I went from one to the other but was absolutely powerless. Nobody cried out or screamed except they all called for water and I had none to give them. I was filled with such horror at their suffering and my inability to help them that I felt that I had suffered some permanent injury to my spirit from which I would never entirely recover." (7)

These men represented just a few of the appalling losses suffered by the British on 12 February. When Wintringham did a head count, the battalion figures were calamitous: of the 600 men under his command at the start of the day only 225 were in any condition to continue the fight. He calculated that of the 400 men who defended the hills 100 had been killed, 100 were wounded, and 75 were missing—stranded on the hills as night fell.

In 1938, *The Book of the Fifteenth International Brigade* gave the "official" version of the first day at Jarama. It admitted mistakes but argued that "it was our very failure to follow the laws of military textbooks that was our glory that day. The stubborn, not-an-inch stand of our men... their refusal to realize when they were beaten—these were the factors which halted the Fascists for the first time in a drive that had been victorious for six successive days."

The homage was more than merited, but that evening there was little sense of triumph let alone pride. The overwhelming feeling in the battalion was one of rage. Many of the volunteers in the Jarama Valley shared Gurney's horror at the slaughter. Morale was shattered almost as completely as the unit itself. According to one survivor, the men were "so edgy, so upset at the whole thing" that they were now "at each others' throats." The volunteers had been sent into battle on the basis of poor intelligence, with faulty equipment, following inadequate training. It should never have happened.

Along the sunken road the British dug in for the night. Very lights—signal flares—whooshed through the night sky and briefly lit up the hills while the occasional clack of gun fire punctuated the silence of the olive groves. The most pitiful sounds of all, though, were the cries of the wounded stranded in no-man's land between the ridge and the sunken road.

At dawn the following day (13 February) the Nationalists renewed their assault. To the relief of the British, however, it was not on their lines but on the northern side of the Morata road defended by volunteers from France, Belgium, and the Balkan Dimitrov Battalion. (8) They fought doggedly during the early morning but were unable to hold their line and were steadily pushed back to positions several hundred meters *behind* Wintringham's men. This meant that the British right flank was exposed. The remnants of no. 4 Company took up a position close to the Morata road, supposedly to fill the gap on the flank, but from mid-afternoon Nationalist artillery began to shell the British with increasing accuracy. No. 4 Company began to retreat, and this rapidly turned into a rout. Once again the company commander Bert Overton buckled. His nerves shattered; he was no longer in control of himself let alone his company. One machine gunner witnessed the men of no. 4 Company "running hell for leather" from the enemy fire with "Overton leading by about 25 yards." Why he had been allowed to remain in command having deserted his men the previous day remains a mystery.

Members of the British Battalion were now falling like dominoes. Without cover from Overton's men, the machine gunners of no. 2 Company were now totally exposed on *their* right flank. The machine gun company was soon outflanked and taken prisoner almost without a shot being fired—although exactly how this happened has been a source of controversy, claim, and counter-claim ever since. The undulating terrain, foreign voices in similar uniforms, the stress of battle, and the lack of food, water, or sleep (many had been awake for some 30 hours now) took their toll on rational decision-making. One gunner saw a Nationalist solider appear about 20 meters in front of him followed by more singing the *Internationale* and shouting *camarada*! with clenched fist salutes. Some in no. 2 Company thought that this must be a mass desertion from the Nationalist lines while others assumed that these Spanish were the long-promised Republican reinforcements who had got ahead of themselves. Once the men realized the deception it was too late, and rebel troops swarmed into the machine gunners' trench. Those who tried to resist or make a run for it were gunned down. The remainder, around 30, were wired together by the wrists and thumbs and marched from the battlefield along the ridge in full sight of their comrades.

On the other side of the valley the prisoners were brought to halt. Company commander Harry Fry was badly injured in the arm, but ironically this probably saved his life. His second in command, Ted Dickinson, managed to rip off Fry's officer insignia—which invited identification and certain death—while bandaging the arm soon after the trench was invaded. Others were not so lucky. Volunteer Phil Elias, from Leeds, asked for—and thought he had been given—permission to smoke. It was a fatal mistake. As he reached into his jacket pocket for the cigarettes, the guard who had given permission riddled his stomach with a burst from his light machine gun. John Stevens, a 21 year old from Islington who was standing beside him, was felled too. When Dickinson, stunned by this brutality, remonstrated with the officer in charge, he was silenced with a bullet in the head.

The rest of the captured men, now terrified, were taken away and held at Talavera, a provincial town on the other side of Madrid. With little food or sanitation they were put to hard labor. Following a "trial" in which there were no translators or defense team, five were condemned to death while 20-year sentences were handed down to the others. The men's case was taken up by the British government on the grounds that executing prisoners contravened the Geneva Convention. Some newspapers took up the campaign too, but not all: the *Daily Mail* huffily described the volunteers as "misguided and hapless communists." In May 1937, however, Fry's men had a stroke of luck. Mussolini demanded the return of some of his Italian officers who had been captured by the Republic, and the Italian dictator put pressure on an unwilling Franco to do a prisoner exchange. Twenty-three of the men were released that month, herded over the border to France by a mob of jeering Falangists, and the others were back in Britain by the end of the year.

The Nationalists now turned the newly captured machine guns toward the sunken road and opened fire on the Battalion HQ. Wintringham reacted quickly to the disaster which was overtaking his men. In what Jason Gurney described as "like some totally improbable incident out of the *Boy's Own Paper*" he ordered the stragglers and survivors grouped around the HQ to fix bayonets and prepare for a counterattack. The idea that "a handful of men could charge more than 200 meters into the face of eight Maxim guns was... futile." Of the 40 or so who tried, just six came back. One of the first to fall was Wintringham himself, felled by a bullet above the knee.

By the evening of the second day of the battle the British Battalion had been savaged again from top to bottom. Hundreds of volunteers now lay dead, and the number of men still in the fight was down to about 150. All the forward positions on the hills had been lost. The leadership had been demolished. The battalion commander and all four company commanders who had led the men into battle the previous day were now out of action. All but one of their heavy machine guns had been captured. The survivors were only holding the line along the sunken road by the most extraordinary mixture of tenacity, luck, and courage. A concerted Nationalist push at this point could have broken that very thin line, but the rebel troops seemed content to hold off—at least until the next day.

On 14 February dawn broke on an exhausted and traumatized British Battalion. Many men had not eaten for three days, nor had they had any proper sleep and water was in short supply. It seemed almost impossible that they would hold out much longer, and yet suddenly there were now two glimmers of hope. First, the promised Spanish reinforcements arrived and dug in on the far left of the British. This offered protection—at last—on the battalion's left flank. Secondly, Jock Cunningham arrived to take command of the battalion in place of the injured Wintringham. Cunningham was revered by many of the men for his gritty resilience, toughness, and experience. He had served as a professional solider with the Argyll and Sutherland Highlanders, and had seen action before Christmas 1936 in both Madrid and Andalucia. Having spent the first two days of the battle in hospital in Morata, laid low by influenza, Cunningham was still sick but his appearance was a real tonic to the other men.

Cunningham ordered the Battalion HQ and line to move back onto the hill behind the sunken road where vines now grow. It was a prudent decision. During the morning the battalion came under increasingly heavy crossfire and a renewed Nationalist advance over the ridge was inevitable. Then, around lunchtime, some of the volunteers heard what they took to be another hopeful sign: the rumble of Russian-made T-26 tanks. They were mistaken. T-26s were indeed advancing up the sunken road from the left, but they were not manned by Republicans.

A T-26 tank used by Republican forces, near Salamanca (Garrapata/ Wikimedia Commons)

They had been captured earlier in the battle and were now in Nationalist hands. The tanks opened fire on the Spanish Republican troops dug in on the left of the sunken road and then began to head toward the British positions. The straight sunken road became, as Cunningham had feared, a death trap.

Without anti-tank guns there were no effective answers to an armored assault. Men retreated as best they could north up the sunken road or through the olive groves. Moroccan infantry advanced behind the tanks to mop up stragglers. No prisoners were taken and the wounded were bayoneted where they lay. New Zealand volunteer Tom Spiller was trying to withdraw when he was grabbed by a wounded man pleading for help. "I had to kick him off... he screamed and roared... of course he could see what was happening only twenty or thirty yards away" where a group of Nationalist soldiers were bayoneting wounded volunteers.

By late afternoon on 14 February the rout was complete, and there was no longer any semblance of a British line as such. Groups of stragglers covered their retreat back over the plateau as best they could. Most headed for the Cookhouse from where they had set off with such high hopes just two days before. By now the scene at the Cookhouse was one of chaos. Apart from the Spanish and British who had been forced back from the front, there were stray Germans, French, and Yugoslavs from the XII International Brigade, which was also in retreat on the other side of the Morata-San Martín road. Wounded men were everywhere and the overriding sense was one of panic. The Nationalists were about to overrun the entire sector—and few expected them to take many prisoners. Either through sheer fear, or under the impression that a general retreat had been ordered, or both, men began to stream down the road to Morata.

At this point General Gal appeared from the XV International Brigade HQ with the Irish commander Frank Ryan. A schoolteachers' son from Limerick and graduate of Trinity College Dublin, Ryan was a charismatic leader and gifted communicator (at university he had won a gold medal for oratory). He was also an experienced military strategist, having been active in the IRA. Along with several other Irish volunteers, Ryan preferred to fight alongside the Americans in the Lincoln Battalion rather than with the "old enemy," the British. He was later taken prisoner and sent to Germany where his ambiguous relationship with the Nazi regime and Eamon de Valera's government of Eire has never been properly explained.

With a mixture of inspirational leadership and naked threats, Jock Cunningham and Frank Ryan managed to impose some order and raise morale. Cajoling, threatening, and pleading, they somehow persuaded the men to haul themselves into one final effort to halt the Nationalist advance. Astonishingly, it worked.

In what has become known as the "Great Rally," around 150 men agreed to return again to the front.

Cunningham and Ryan led the column up the hill from the Cookhouse. At the junction with the Morata-San Martín road they swung left, heading once again for the sunken road and the Nationalist lines. Ryan recalled that they set off in silence, perhaps resigned to their fate or weary beyond caring. He realized that he needed to do something fast and recalled a trick from his old days in the IRA when holding a banned demonstration. "Sing up, ye sons o' guns!" he shouted and began a rendition of the *Internationale*. Gradually the song was taken up by the entire column so that the "unshaven, unkempt, blood-stained, grimy" band of men held clenched fists in the air and became "full of fight again." John "Bosco" Jones recalled, "I'll never forget it… we were stone mad when I think about it. As we moved up troops from all around, Spaniards and others, rallied. And we found ourselves in a small army!"

Cunningham led the troops onto the plateau but with darkness falling misjudged the distance, leaving them well short of the sunken road. This meant that the volunteers were now sandwiched between the Nationalist frontline and support line. (9) When the volunteers opened fire on the rebel positions there was total confusion in the dark. One described the action as "a shambles… I did not know whether I was coming or going. There were flashes all around me left right and center." The skirmishing went on for some hours but the rebel units were caught completely unawares. They assumed that they were at the center of some new Republican counteroffensive, led by fresh troops, and panicked in the half dark. Terrified of being cut off from their support lines by a pincer movement, Nationalist troops fled over the plateau, back across the sunken road and to the safety of the hills—White House, Suicide, and Conical—where they had started the day. It was an extraordinary outcome. The remains of the British Battalion had just routed some of Franco's finest troops on the verge of breaking through to the Valencia road and a decisive victory. That same night (14-15 February), fresh Spanish troops arrived from Madrid. These reinforcements dug in along the front and the Republican line was sealed. The rebels never again came as close to breaking the Republicans in this sector until the end of the war.

*

The American Abraham Lincoln Battalion was among Republican reinforcements now being drafted into the Jarama Valley. The first volunteers from the United States left New York on Christmas Day 1936, and this was their first battle. Led by 28-year-old Robert Merriman, a lumberjack's son who had worked his way up to a lectureship at the University of California and who was in Europe on an agricultural research scholarship when the war broke out, there were about 400 Lincolns. A large number of the US volunteers at Jarama were also students, innocent perhaps compared to their European comrades who had already experienced the rough edge of fascism, but no less courageous. The Lincolns moved into the trenches on 23 February and saw action almost immediately when they were ordered to break the by now well entrenched Nationalist line. A storm of fire met the Americans as they charged west through the olive groves and across the open ground known at the Cerro Pingarrón. What was supposed to have been part of a bigger offensive was in fact backed only by a pair of RussianT-26 tanks. As a consequence the assault failed but not before 20 men had been killed and nearly 60 wounded. (10)

Skirmishing continued during the following days and then, on 27 February, the Lincolns were ordered to spearhead a Republican offensive intended to push the nationalists off the Pingarrón heights and back over the Jarama river. This assault, too, was a catastrophic failure and resulted in the wholly needless deaths of many scores of Americans. When Merriman questioned the sense of the order to attack, he was told by Colonel Vladimir Copic, a Yugoslav commander of the XV Brigade, that the Pingarrón was to be taken "at all costs" and that he—Merriman—would be court-martialed along with others if they did not obey the order. Once again, the Lincolns were promised support which never appeared. Merriman was felled by a shot which cracked his shoulder blade into five pieces as soon as he left the trenches, and he was just one of many casualties. Of the 263 men who went into action that day, only 150 survived. Ernest Hemingway described Copic's order as "monumental stupidity," and many of the Lincolns suspected that it was based on the commander's vanity rather than any calculated assessment of the odds. One survivor joked with grim humor that the brigade was named after Lincoln because he too had been assassinated.

Irish volunteers mixed in with the Lincolns also suffered heavy losses, including their 21-year-old commander Charlie Donnelly, who was killed as his unit withdrew from the deadly mayhem on 27 February. According to one volunteer who was there, Donnelly was "crouched behind an olive tree. He has picked up a bunch of olives from the ground and is squeezing them. I hear him say quietly, between a lull of machine-gun fire 'Even the olives are bleeding...' A bullet got him square in the temple a few minutes later." (11)

Thereafter neither side could break through. The Nationalist forces had gained some 20 square kilometers of territory but had not severed or captured the Valencia road. It was a failure, however, which depressed the spirit of the Republicans as much as the Nationalists as both sides now understood that this would be a long war. The front remained largely as it was established in mid-February 1937 until the end of the conflict more than two years later. As in the trench stalemate of World War I, there were continuous night patrols, sniping, and raiding parties. For the most part, though, the sector was relatively quiet. In the spring of 1937 writers Ernest Hemingway and Martha Gellhorn went to visit the front and the wounded American volunteers in

Republican troops celebrate Christmas 1937 with a meal of paella at San Martín de la Vega. (Mesón El Cid)

Morata. By then the zone was so untroubled that they were able to move freely behind the line and enjoy a picnic lunch.

Apart from the Nationalist snipers the volunteers faced various enemies. Boredom was one of them as men spent many long weeks on the inactive but still dangerous front. The International Brigade volunteers could not, of course, go home like the Spanish troops and complained loudly about not being given leave even to visit Madrid. The food was poor, consisting largely of coffee, chickpeas, sardines, bread, and rice. Insanitary conditions rapidly encouraged rats and lice—an enemy which seemed to survive despite daily assaults by the volunteers. In the early summer of 1937 to break the monotony the British volunteers constructed a giant stone clenched fist to the comrades who had fallen. This was destroyed by the Nationalists in 1939, but the remains can still be seen. (12) On the opposite hill a new sculpture known as the Monument to Solidarity has been erected by the Morata de Tajuña town council. There are also some very well preserved trenches on this hill. (13)

Even today, the exact death toll of the Battle of Jarama is unknown. Oxford historian Hugh Thomas estimated that along the valley there were over 10,000 Republican casualties: 1,000 dead, 7,000 wounded, and 3,500 sick. The Nationalists suffered around 6,000 casualties. Given these figures and the importance of the battle, it is disappointing that so little has been done to commemorate the conflict in the Jarama Valley. There is a small memorial in the municipal cemetery, erected in the 1980s, to those in the Brigades who fell. (14) A remarkable and honorable exception is the Mesón El Cid restaurant/museum—a local initiative and essential for finding out more about the battle. (15)

The best way to really understand what happened at Jarama, however, is by walking along the sunken road. Even today debris from 80 years ago can be found in the surrounding fields, and the scars of the war are visible on the hillsides. In the quiet olive groves beside the track, some of the volunteers still lie in unmarked graves where they fell. It is here that the indomitable spirit of the International Brigadiers can be captured on the breeze from the valley and in the song that immortalized their fight:

There's a valley in Spain called Jarama
It's a valley we all know so well
It's the place where we fought against the Fascists
And saw that peaceful valley turned to hell (16)

Visiting Jarama

The battlefield site of the Jarama Valley is some 30 kilometers to the southeast of Madrid—by car the journey takes around 35 minutes. Any of the places listed below can be visited as separate sites. However, for a full exploration of the site, the following route is suggested. This itinerary takes approximately five or six hours, including journey time to and from Madrid, lunch, and a look around the museum.

Suggested Route

Start: The farmhouse called Venta de Frascuelo (known during the battle as the Cookhouse), Calle del Baja Azotea, Morata de Tajuña. (1)

To reach the Venta de Frascuelo, take the A3 highway out of Madrid, direction Valencia. Pass the town called Rivas Vaciamadrid, which is on the A3, some 20 kilometers out of Madrid. Then take the exit on the right marked Salida 21 towards Chinchón. Follow the M832 road in a straight line. Take the second exit at the roundabout where the M832 leads into the M311. Follow the ascending, winding road until you come to a T-junction with the M302 (the Morata de Tajuña-San Martín road). Turn left, following the sign to Morata de Tajuña. Then take the first right after some 250 meters. This is a continuation of the M311 and also known on some maps as the Calle Baja Azotea. The road descends steeply, and the Venta de Frascuelo farmhouse is on the right hand side of the road after a sharp left bend about 1.5 kilometers down.

Leaving the Venta de Frascuelo farmhouse, return back up the hill on the M311 (Calle de Baja Azotea). At the top turn left onto the M302 (Calle de Asilo), direction San Martín de la Vega.

Follow the M302 for about 2 kilometers to the sunken road, an unmade dirt road between the olive groves. Turn left from the M302 onto the sunken road. After about 700 meters the olive groves end, and the road divides into three. Take the right-hand track and park. This is the site of the Memorial to the International Brigades. (4)

From here there is a panoramic view over the hills where the British Battalion fought. Be aware that these hills are private land and are used for hunting during the season. The sunken road is a public right of way and there are remains from the Civil War on either side.

Leaving the International Brigades Memorial, return along the sunken road to the M302. Turn right. After 700 meters

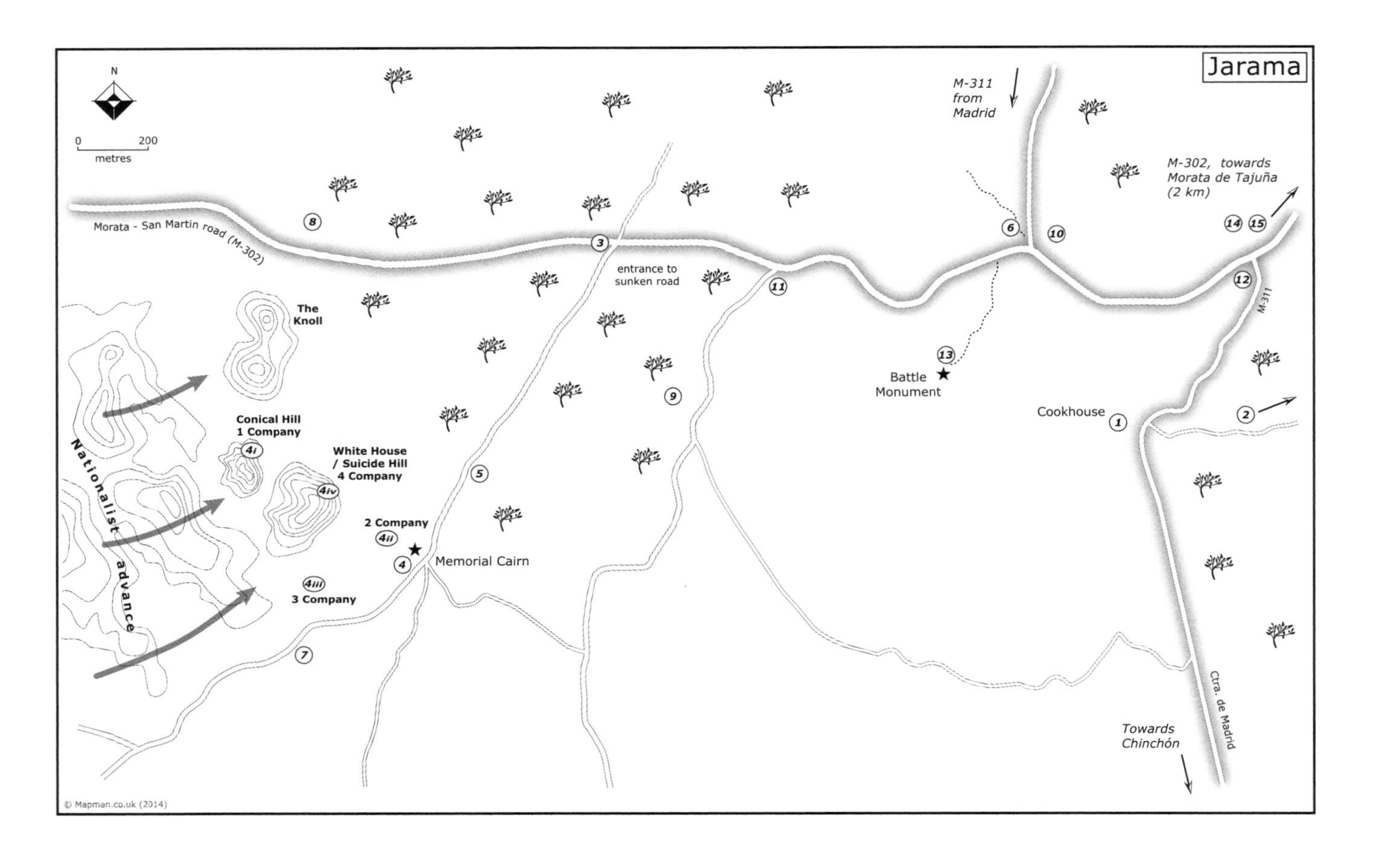
Jarama
N
0
200
metres
M-311
from
Madrid
M-302, towards
Morata de Tajuña
(2 km)
Morata - San Martin road (M-302)
entrance to
sunken road
M-311
The
Knoll
Conical Hill
1 Company
White House
/ Suicide Hill
4 Company
2 Company
3 Company
Memorial Cairn
Battle
Monument
Cookhouse
Nationalist advance
Ctra. de Madrid
Towards
Chinchón
1
2
3
4
4i
4ii
4iii
4iv
5
6
7
8
9
10
11
12
13
14
15
© Mapman.co.uk (2014)

there is a dirt track leading off on the right. Pull in and park here to see the small Memorial to the Lincoln Battalion. (11) Looking back down the M302 to the left is the area which was fought over during the "Great Rally" on 14/15 February. (9)

Continue along the M302 to the Monument to Solidarity, which is clearly visible on a hillock as the road descends. Turn right and park below the monument. The path up to the monument passes clear remains of zigzag trenches and there are deep trenches at the top of the hill. (13)

Leave the monument site and turn right onto the M302 into Morata.

At the Mesón El Cid is the Museo Batalla Jarama (Battle of Jarama Musuem, Calle del Carmen 36, Morata de Tajuña). (15)

Route Notes

(1) Venta de Frascuelo farmhouse. This building, known to the British as the Cookhouse, is still there and looks much as it did 80 years ago in contemporary accounts by the British volunteers. It currently opens at weekends as a small farm market and is well worth looking around to soak up the atmosphere.

(2) Morata de Tajuña is clearly visible four kilometers away from the Cookhouse. The town was used as a supply base for frontline troops and a medical center for the wounded, and was the nearest center of rest and recuperation for those on leave. Morata was frequently bombed from the air in Nationalist raids.

(3) The "sunken road" is off the main M302 (shown on some maps as the Calle Asilo) road between Morata de Tajuña and San Martín de la Vega. It is an unmade road which runs between olive groves and it is not signed. As you enter the sunken road note the remains of a Nationalist bunker some ten meters into the olive grove on the right hand side. Other remains can be found on the other side of the M302.

(4) The small Memorial to the International Brigades is about

600 meters down the sunken road on the right hand side. From here there is a clear view over the valley and the positions where the volunteers fought. White House Hill is on the left and the adjoining Suicide Hill is center left. Conical Hill is just beyond. The Knoll stands on its own some 500 meters to the right (northwest) of Conical Hill. The British line stretched from The Knoll in the north by the Morata-San Martín road (M302) across the hillocks to the south. From this vantage point it is also possible to get an idea of the positions of the British companies on the first day as referred to in the text. On the sloping ground beneath the cairn, on the right hand side of the path which leads down, it is still possible to see the remains of fox-holes dug by Nationalist troops.

(4i) position of no. 1 Company (Conway's) on first day;
(4ii) position of no. 2 Company (Fry's) on first day;
(4iii) position of no. 3 Company (Briskey's) on first day;
(4iv) position of no. 4 Company (Overton's) on first day.

(5) Probable position of the British Battalion HQ for the first two days of the battle.

(6) Position of the XV International Brigade HQ.

(7) Possible position of the hollow where Gurney found the 50 forgotten wounded.

(8) Franco-Belgian Battalion (also called 6 February Battalion) and Dimitrov Battalion positions.

(9) Area between Nationalist front and support line where the XV International Brigade attacked after the "Great Rally."

(10) Lincoln Battalion arrival point on their first day.

(11) Point from which Lincoln Battalion attacked on 23 February, now marked by a small cairn.

(12) Remains of a memorial to the Jarama dead at the junction of the M311 and M302. The original sculpture was built by the

Republicans and International Brigadiers. The statue, in the form of a large clenched fist crafted by Eduardo Carretero, was destroyed by the Nationalists in 1939. The unmarked graves of both Spanish and International Brigade dead probably lie around the base.

(13) Monument to Solidarity: this sculpture in bronze of two fists clasped together dominates the hillside and gives a great view of the valleys of the Jarama and Tajuña rivers. It was sculpted by Martin Chirino and unveiled by the Mayoress of Morata de Tajuña in 2006. It is frequently daubed with slogans by radical Nationalists who cannot tolerate its presence. The trenches here were never part of the frontline, but built as reserve trenches with the help of labor from Morata in 1937.

The Monument to Solidarity on the Jarama battlefield
(James Ferguson)

(14) Morata de Tajuña cemetery, Calle del Cementerio, Morata. The small memorial to the fallen volunteers is on the far wall opposite the main gate. Enter through the main gate and walk directly ahead to the far wall, then turn right and walk another 15 meters.

(15) Mesón El Cid, Calle del Carmen 36, Morata de Tajuña. The Civil War museum attached to this restaurant (*mesón*) is an essential stop on the trip. The curator and founder is a local who has spent the past 60 years collecting a bewildering variety of objects from the battlefield. There are fascinating photographs and artifacts as well as displays of weaponry and other Civil War objects. A set menu lunch here is also highly recommended: the homemade food is excellent value.

(16) The song *Jarama Valley* has been recorded by many artists including Woody Guthrie and Pete Seeger. They can be found on YouTube. Another excellent song about the battle is called *Viva la Quinta Brigada* by the Irish folksinger Christy Moore.

The Jarama battlefield museum in Morata de Tajuña contains an extraordinary cornucopia of items collected from the front. (James Ferguson)

7

HEMINGWAY'S WAR: GUADARRAMA, VALLE DE LOS CAÍDOS, AND EL ESCORIAL

"My brother was a pilot
And received a map one day
He packed his things into a box
And headed southward on his way

My brother is a conqueror
Our people need the space
To gain more ground and territory
Is the age old longing of our race

The space my brother conquered
Is in the Guadarrama peaks
The length is six foot two
And nigh on four feet deep"
Bertolt Brecht, 1938 (author's translation)

The American author Ernest Hemingway probably did more than any other writer to bring the tragedy of the Spanish Civil War home to a mass audience outside Spain. As a journalist in Madrid, Hemingway spent prolonged periods reporting from the city under siege. He subsequently used the experience as the basis for his prophetic novel, *For Whom the Bell Tolls,* which warned of the fascist menace engulfing Europe. It is widely regarded as one of the finest war stories of the twentieth century; President Barack Obama is just one reader who lists the book among those which have most influenced him.

This chapter and the accompanying tour aims to uncover the truth behind Hemingway's powerful fiction. The novel is set in the Sierra de Guadarrama, the spectacular mountain range clearly visible from the center of Madrid. It was here that Nationalist columns advancing on the capital were held in the mountain passes, and the resistance of the civilian militia was crucial to the defense of the Republic. Had the rebel troops broken the opposition, Franco's army would have taken Madrid within days.

Both sides constructed elaborate trenches and dug-outs—one Republican commander called them the "most important series of fortifications in the war"—and even today the vestiges of war still scar the hillsides. The walking tours follow a path through an area that has been designated as one of outstanding natural beauty, rated by many hikers among the best walking country in Europe. It is a haunting and unforgettable backdrop to a pivotal episode of the Civil War.

The tour also covers two other monuments in the *sierra* which are highly relevant to the Civil War: General Franco's tomb and King Philip II's palace at San Lorenzo de El Escorial, a town which also features in *For Whom the Bell Tolls.* The three locations can be visited in one day or as separate trips, but in combination they help unlock a deeper understanding of the conflict and the dictatorship which followed.

*

Ernest Hemingway visited Madrid before, during, and after the Civil War; he said that one of the things he would regret about dying is that he would never again be able to enjoy a drink in the bars of the city. He was commissioned by the North American News Alliance (NANA) to cover the war as a news reporter and made various trips from Madrid to the Guadarrama front. A stellar writer of his generation, Hemingway was also one of the best paid. He pocketed a fee of $500 for each cabled story—around ten times more than most NANA reporters were paid—and $1,000 for his longer dispatches sent by mail. Not surprisingly, at these rates he was a regular filing copy from the Telefonica building in the center of Madrid while in the evenings he and his mistress, the writer Martha Gellhorn, were at the center of an active coterie at the nearby Hotel Florida (see Chapter 3).

The war suited Hemingway's macho approach to life and he rapidly jettisoned any attempt to remain objective; in the *sierra* he helped the untrained militiamen master the rifles which they had been supplied with. At the end of April 1937, in his last NANA report from Madrid, Hemingway described climbing and trekking for hours on horseback "to important positions 4,800 feet high in the Guadarrama mountains." Once at the front Hemingway was transported in an armored car which came under attack from Nationalist fire, the bullets pinging loudly on the metal plating. He met a tough guerrilla leader called *El Guerrero* (the warrior) who explained how, despite his company having been wiped out several times in desperate fighting through the mountain gullies, a constant stream of fresh recruits had held off the Nationalist advance over the winter. And not all the guerrillas were men. Hemingway was introduced to a young woman combatant while *El Guerrero* explained that his own wife, who had fought throughout the winter, had only recently returned to Madrid because she was heavily pregnant.

There is no doubt that Hemingway hyped up some of his NANA copy, but his experiences around Guadarrama were important because they also provided the background to his novel *For Whom the Bell Tolls.* The book's tight plot and prophetic, anti-fascist message made it an instant bestseller and an enduring work of fiction.

Its hero, Robert Jordan, is an American anti-fascist who joins a band of gypsy partisans living and fighting in the mountains—Jordan and the gypsies are tasked with supporting a major

Republican offensive. Hemingway's fiction is rooted in fact: the real offensive, known as the Battle of La Granja, was launched at the end of May 1937. The attack was an utter failure and cost the Republicans dear in terms of men and materiel.

Hemingway also used several other locations in the *sierra,* such as El Escorial, to anchor the novel in reality. One night, for example, Jordan and the gypsy leader Pablo hear German bombers in the dark sky overhead, but in greater numbers than they have ever heard them before. "It is bad, Robert Jordan thought. This is really bad." Jordan's mind races as he tries to work out the bombers' target. Are they about to attack the Republican lines in the *sierra*? The planes pass over and Jordan begins to time them. "He looked at his watch. By now they should be over the lines, the first ones anyway. He pushed the knob that set the second hand to clicking and watched it move around. No, perhaps not yet. By now. Yes. Well over by now. Two hundred and fifty miles an hour for those one-elevens anyway… The shadows of the Heinkels moving over the land as the shadows of sharks pass over a sandy floor of the ocean. There was no bump, bump, bumping thud of bombs. His watch ticked on. They're going on… to Escorial, or to the flying field at Manzanares el Real, he thought."

Yet for all its literary merit, *For Whom the Bell Tolls* is a work of fiction. So what are the facts?

General Mola's March

When the rebel generals declared their *coup d'état* on 18 July 1936, they expected the garrison at the Montaña Barracks in Madrid to join the uprising, supported by troops from the north of Spain led by General Emilio Mola. This did not happen and the *coup* failed (see Chapter Four). Mola expected to be the first rebel commander to arrive in the capital when his troops left from their base in Burgos, some 300 kilometers to the north of Madrid. Burgos is the city of El Cid, who led the Christians to expel the Muslims from Spain. With its starting point in a deeply conservative city in the heart of Castile, Mola's march fitted into a convenient, quasi-historical nationalist narrative about a crusade against godlessness. The professional rebel soldiers were also joined by Falangist volunteers and other monarchist troops (known as Carlists) from the northern province of Navarra.

The highway between Madrid and Burgos was an important artery connecting the capital with the north of Spain. About 45 kilometers to the north of Madrid, the road threads its way through the peaks of the Sierra de Guadarrama. This impressive mountain range runs for hundreds of kilometers around the north and west of the city, offering Madrid a natural defensive barrier. One traveler awed by the magnitude of the *sierra* was the British author Laurie Lee. In his 1969 memoir *As I Walked Out One Midsummer Morning,* he describes traveling across Spain on foot in the months before the outbreak of the Civil War. As he hiked across the Castilian plain from Segovia the *sierra* began to loom up "till it filled half the sky—the immense east-west barrier of the Guadarramas." It took Lee two days to cross the range, during which time "gulping the fine dry air and sniffing the pitch pine mountains I was perhaps never so alive and so alone again." Then, as he crossed the pass, he saw before him "a new country emerge—the immense plain of La Mancha, stretching flat as cowhide and smudged like a sore with distant Madrid." The 19-year-old Lee subsequently joined the International Brigades. Had he returned to the *sierra* he would have found himself far from alone, but in one of the most important theaters of the war.

The pass though the mountains on the Burgos road is called Somosierra and was long recognized as a strategic stronghold against hostile forces. It was here, for example, that the citizens of Madrid put up a stand against Napoleon's army when it marched on the city in November 1808. As soon as it became known that the Nationalist force was heading south in July 1936, militiamen from Madrid once again rushed to the Somosierra pass. The Burgos road was a vital conduit to the city and, crucially, a nearby reservoir supplied Madrid with fresh water: had the reservoir fallen into Nationalist hands, taps in the capital would have run dry within days.

As a popular destination for summer excursions, many *Madrileños* knew the *sierra* well, and initially holding the Nationalists there was done without significant casualties. Republican militiamen traveled easily between the city and the mountain pass, bringing reinforcements and supplies. The Nationalist army, too, swelled in numbers as more troops arrived from Burgos. The battle intensified, and the two sides fought each other to a standstill. Frustrated by the failure to push through the Somosierra pass, rebel commanders rapidly looked for alternative routes over the mountains into Madrid. To the west, the road snaking its way through the Puerto de Guadarrama pass, above the mountain town of Guadarrama, was next on their list.

Republican militiamen and women attack Nationalist positions at Somosierra, near Guadarrama. (Google Art Project)

Puerto de Guadarrama, Path to Madrid

The importance of the mountain pass known as the Puerto de Guadarrama has been understood for centuries. There has been a carriageway over the mountains here since Roman times, but with a radical upgrade in the late eighteenth century the road became a crucial link between central and northwest Spain. The strategic significance of the road soon became evident too: when Napoleon's troops marched on Madrid, the pass was one of those they used to reach the city, although they had to overcome several setbacks. On Christmas Eve 1808, a column of French infantry trudged up the mountain pass in a blinding snowstorm. The officers' horses slid from under them and cannons refused to budge. Then bands of Spanish *bandolero* guerrillas appeared on the hillsides and began to take pot-shots at them. Finally the hapless column retreated back down the pass until the weather lifted. The pass was also the point at which Spain's two central regions—Castilla la Vieja and Castilla la Nueva (Old and New Castile)—met. A statue of a lion was erected to mark the highest spot when the road was opened in the 1770s. The statue, still on its plinth pockmarked by the war and sitting in the middle of the dusty road, gave the area its name, Alto del León (Lion Heights). The lion was chosen as a symbol of Spain's imperial glory—the globes under its paws were intended to symbolize the country's hold over Europe and Latin America.

It was around the Alto del León that one of the first important battles of the Civil War took place. The Puerto de Guadarrama was one of the few gateways between Madrid and the north of Spain, and the Alto del León was the key. When the uprising was declared both sides moved quickly. The military garrison in Valladolid, the capital of Old Castile, had immediately declared for the Nationalists. A column of soldiers left Valladolid on 20 July and headed for Madrid. The column was led by Colonel Emilio Serrador and included regular infantry, Civil Guards, and a contingent of young Falangists.

The present-day Alto del León, with the bar-restaurant Asador Alto del León in the background (Miguel753/Wikimedia Commons)

The arrival of rebel troops had, however, been anticipated by the government, which had sent a force to occupy the Puerto de Guadarrama and Alto del León the previous day (21 July). Around 450 regular soldiers who had remained loyal to the Republic were gathered together with a few hundred civilian militiamen. The force was under the command of Colonel Enrique del Castillo, an officer who had also stood by his oath of allegiance to the elected government. These ground troops also had some air support from half a dozen small bombers.

The Nationalist column arrived at the Alto del León at around midday, and the two sides began bloody skirmishing which went on for the next six hours, with the Nationalist force launching a full frontal attack on Republican positions. The road was rapidly churned up by shelling, which made the use of motorized armored support difficult, and the July sun beat down mercilessly. One

Nationalist combatant recalled the "pine trees scorched by bursts of fire, the fumes from gunpowder choking our parched throats, and the sun of the *Sierra* which burned almost as much as the deadly bombs launched from the planes."

The battle for control of the pass went on throughout the blazing hot afternoon; hand-to-hand fighting turned the craggy rocks and pine forest into a lethal maze, and casualties were heavy. By around 6PM the Nationalists were on top—literally—of the Alto del León as the inexperienced civilian militia began to crumble. "Cries of 'Viva España!' and 'Onward Spain!' rang out as a final push was made through blood, dirt, and mountains of wounded," recalled one of the rebels. The statue of the lion was draped with the Falangists' flag. The role played by their vanguard in the storming of the heights was subsequently commemorated by a subtle name change. Under the Franco dictatorship, the Alto del León (singular) became the Alto de los Leones (the Lions' Heights) in honor of the young Falangists, the Lions of Castile, who fought here.

The cost of the action to the Nationalists in terms of human life was dear: nearly 100 were left dead or badly wounded. Precise figures for Republican losses are not known but they were heavy, and what happened next is unclear. According to some versions, both Colonel Castillo and his son were killed, heroically, in the fighting around the Alto del León. There is, however, a far less savory version of events. Many of the militiamen were dazed and embittered by the loss of life. Colonel Castillo was made a scapegoat and blamed for the rout. He was escorted to the nearby town of Guadarrama for a summary trial in which both he and his son were accused of being closet Nationalists who had ordered militiamen into the line of fire and deliberately engineered defeat: they were pronounced guilty and shot. Was this Nationalist propaganda designed to cast the Republicans in a bad light? Maybe, but it is certainly true that many militia were highly suspicious of the professional army officers who remained loyal to the Republic. In the tense, confused weeks following the uprising, there were documented cases of militia turning on officers who they believed had betrayed them in battle. Not surprisingly, there was an increase in the flow of army officers initially loyal to the Republic deserting to the Nationalist side.

Control of the Alto del León was an important tactical gain for the rebels. It did not, however, present them with an open route into Madrid. The winding road which descends from the heights was still in government hands and strongly defended by Republicans. Although heavily shelled—one observer calculated that around three-quarters of the buildings were reduced to rubble—the town of Guadarrama remained an important Republican base. Within a few days resistance was further bolstered by the arrival of a detachment from the legendary communist 5th Regiment. Under their charismatic commanders Enrique Líster and Valentín González (known as *El Campesino*, or the peasant), the Fifth Regiment was well trained and observed strict communist discipline. The volunteers were allowed to elect their NCOs and officers but, once chosen, their orders had to be obeyed. This was Lenin's democratic centralism in military form, and there was no chance that any officer of the 5th Regiment would suffer the same fate as Colonel Castillo at the hands of aggrieved militiamen. Journalist Geoffrey Cox, who covered the war for the *News Chronicle*, said that the mountain terrain "suited the Fifth Regiment perfectly... It was here that the rebels learned to respect them as enemies."

Fierce skirmishing around the Alto del León went on through August 1936. Mikhail Koltsov, a shady correspondent for the Soviet newspaper *Pravda*, reported that

> the fighting goes on among the rocks, gullies, and woodland. There is not a day of truce. The fascists are magnetized by the proximity of the capital just 50 km away. If they can get down onto the plain they can

> strangle Madrid, the government, the Republic. The Republicans know that. They know the cost of the slightest error or mistake.

But errors there were. With men spread out across the pine-clad slopes, it was often hard to distinguish friend from foe, and there were lethal cases of mistaken identity. One of the best-known was the tragic end of Josep Sunyol, a Catalan member of parliament, leading Republican, and President of Barcelona Football Club. On 6 August Sunyol was on the road up the Guadarrama pass to the Alto del León. He wanted to see the front for himself and boost the morale of the loyalist troops. Sunyol and his party were heading for some of the high ground which they thought was in Republican hands. Yet unknown to them, it had been lost to a Nationalist push earlier in the day. When Sunyol saw a group of soldiers, he got out of the car and approached them with the Republican greeting, *Salud!* Only then did he realize his mistake: the troops were Nationalist. Sunyol was summarily executed there and then, along with the three other members of his party. It is not known exactly where Sunyol died, but the event is now marked with a small headstone in a park on the outskirts of Guadarrama on the road leading up to the Alto del León.

Although they could make no further gain down the pass toward the town of Guadarrama, the Nationalists began to consolidate the ground which they held. Their lines stretched some two kilometers on either side of the Alto del León. Beyond that, however, they were hemmed in by the Republicans. Official daily military despatches from both sides through the autumn of 1936 tell the story of a war of attrition: "4 October Our artillery shell enemy positions in the pass of Guadarrama without them returning fire… 8 October all quiet along the Guadarrama front… 13 October our batteries in Guadarrama shelled enemy positions… 27 October our batteries exchanged fire with the enemy for several hours without any important consequences for our part…"

Alto del León with road leading down towards San Rafael. Note the smoke from artillery fire on the hillside (center). (Biblioteca Nacional de España, fondo fotográfico de la guerra civil española)

One Republican raid was led by the 28-year-old Italian socialist Fernando De Rosa, who had already been at the center of a major international rumpus. In October 1929 De Rosa had attempted to assassinate the Italian Crown Prince Umberto of Piedmont, a commander in Mussolini's army, while the prince was on a visit to Belgium. The trial became an international *cause célèbre*. Defended by a smart lawyer called Paul-Henri Spaak, who later became the Belgian premier and first Secretary General of the United Nations, the young socialist was given a very lenient sentence. Mussolini was outraged, and the diplomatic spat spiraled into an international war of words about the nature of fascism. In early October 1936, De Rosa led an assault on Nationalist positions around the Heights del León, but was killed within seconds of leaving his dug-out.

And so the night raids, skirmishes, and sorties went on. In Hemingway's *For Whom the Bell Tolls,* Jordan recalls a sortie during those early days. "The fascists had attacked and we stopped them on that slope in the grey rocks, the scrub pines and the gorse of the Guadarrama hill sides" as the Nationalists came "sifting down between the rocks and through the trees."

Then, as autumn turned into winter, a new enemy bore down on both sides: the cold. At between 1,500 and 2,000 meters above sea level, the temperatures in the *sierra* can drop to -20ºC during the winter months. Both Nationalists and Republicans formed ski companies: the communist 5th Regiment, for example, formed a special Batallón Alpino (Alpine Battalion) and increased numbers with a recruitment drive among ski club members.

As the war went on, mountain peaks around the Alto del León were taken, lost, and retaken. The peak closest to the Heights of Leon on the southwestern side is called the Cabeza Líjar. It is the point at which the provinces of Avila, Segovia, and Madrid meet. The summit is now capped with a concrete viewing platform, or *mirador,* built on an old Civil War bunker. A path leading to the *mirador* passes the remains of frontline observation posts, and the views from the top are breathtaking. The strategic importance of Cabeza Líjar is evident, not least because it overlooks the Alto del León. It was initially held by the Republicans, but they were knocked off the peak in September 1936. Several attempts were made to retake it—but without success.

In May 1937, for example, the Republicans launched an offensive which they hoped would break the Nationalist line in the *sierra.* This was known as the Battle of La Granja, and preparations for the push are central to the plot of *For Whom the Bell Tolls.* Storming the Cabeza Líjar formed part of the operation although, without overstatement, one Republican commander, Mañuel Tagueña, later wrote, "we knew this would not be easy." He recalled the "titanic" effort of using oxen to lug guns and ammunition up the hillsides of what is now the Valle de los Caídos. The peak opposite the Cabeza Líjar, known as the

View from the summit of the Cabeza Líjar, with Guadarrama town and Madrid in the distance (Rubén Ojeda/Wikimedia Commons)

Summit of Salamanca, was occupied by the Republicans. The night before the attack, men, mortars, and machine guns took up forward positions under cover of darkness and in absolute silence so as not to alert the enemy. Tagueña described the attack: "I will never forget dawn that day. Suddenly the whole summit of the Cabeza Líjar lit up in a huge flash as we unleashed a storm of rifle and machine gun fire." The Republicans overran the advanced positions but, despite repeated attempts, could not dislodge the rebel position on the summit. Tagueña gave orders for his men to hold back so that the Republican mortars could be brought into action. "Unfortunately, the battery commander was an old sergeant who had a magnificent beard but not much technical knowledge." The initial rounds were poorly sighted "and some of the missiles fell on our own lines." The aim was soon adjusted so that "black explosions from the grenades rose up on the summit of the Cabeza Líjar... but we were never able to occupy it."

Republican disillusionment was matched by Nationalist frustration. The march on the pass at the Alto del León should have led to the gates of Madrid and a quick victory. But once again the rebel army was checked, their ambition thwarted by Republican courage and the fearsome terrain of the *sierra.* As the war ground on, the focus of the conflict moved to other sectors; in the mountains both sides became more entrenched, but neither force had the strength of numbers to break the other. The two front lines stretched across the mountain sides in unbroken deadlock until the Republican war effort collapsed at the end of March 1939.

VISITING ALTO DEL LEÓN

The site and remains of the battle for the Guadarrama pass around the Alto del León are easily accessible today. Start from outside a bar-restaurant called the Asador Alto del León, located at the highest point of the pass and clearly marked by the statue of the lion in the middle of the road. The bar-restaurant is a good place to stop for a coffee, drink, or lunch.

The Alto del León is 57 kilometers outside Madrid. By car: take the A6 direction A Coruña. Take the exit 52 onto the N-VI and follow directions to San Rafael. There is a large, free car park by the side of the road next to the Asador Alto del León. By bus: there is a regular return bus service from Madrid *intercambiador* (bus/metro station) Moncloa to Guadarrama. The bus number is 664 and there is a stop in the central square of Guadarrama. It is then necessary to take a taxi (journey time 10 minutes) to the Alto del León. The taxi rank is opposite the *ayuntamiento* (town hall) in the square. The local number for the taxi rank is: 91 854 10 07.

Immediately behind the Asador Alto del León is a concrete former Nationalist observation post. However, there are many more sights of interest within a short walk; on the opposite side of the road from the restaurant are well preserved trenches and blockhouses. This route follows the officially designated footpath called the GR10.

The route is easy walking over a route of five or six kilometers along an unmade road and forest path. The differential in gradient is around 80 meters. No special equipment is necessary, but sensible footwear should be worn. It is advisable to wear a hat and take some water in summer.

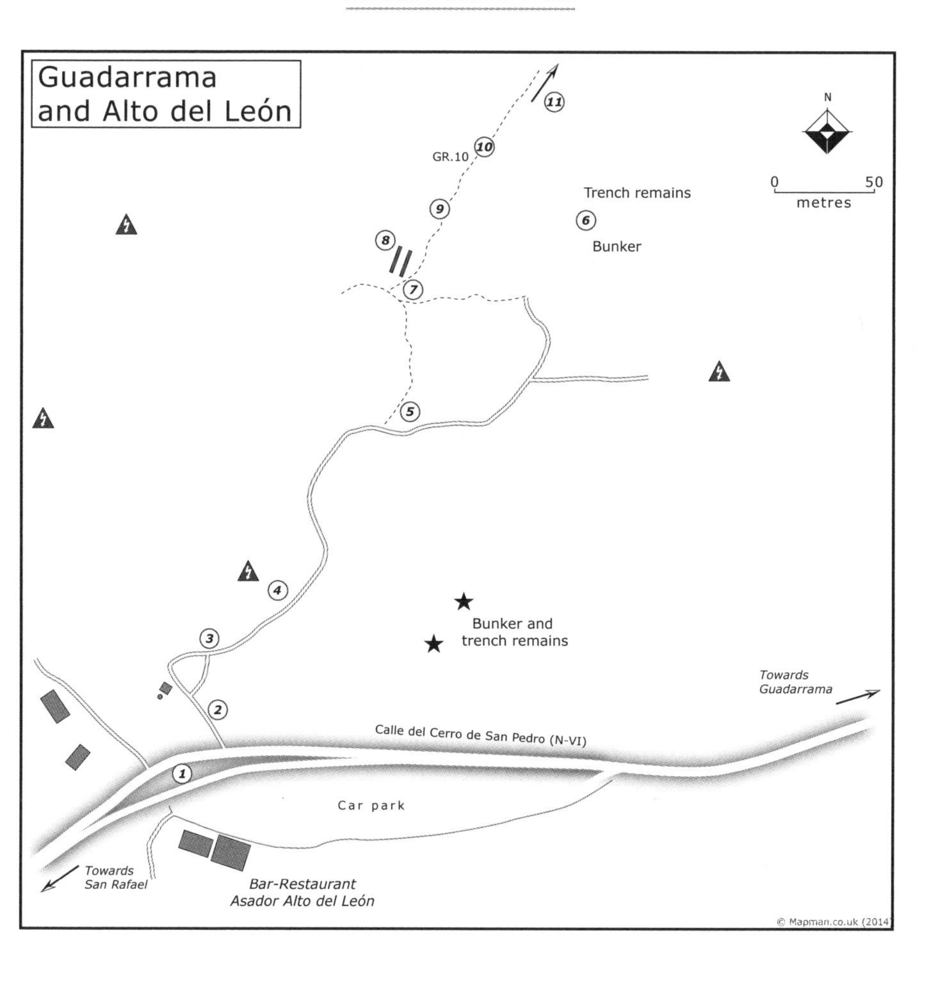

(1) Cross by the lion statue in the center of the road.
(2) Take the path immediately leading up the slope which has a fence on the right hand side.
(3) About 20 meters up from the road there is a green iron gate which leads to an unmade road on the other side of the fence. Go through this gate and walk up another 20 meters to the unmade road.
(4) Follow the unmade road up. Pass the electricity pylon which is on the left about 100 meters from the gate.

Remains of a Nationalist bunker built into the rocks near the Alto del León (James Ferguson)

(5) Follow the curve of the road round the right and then to the left for another 250 meters to the top of the slope. There is a red and white communications mast on rocks at the top of the slope.
(6) A concrete bunker with a barrel-shaped roof built into the rocks can be seen about 50 meters from the red and white mast. This was a Nationalist position. It is possible to enter the bunker and see exactly what Nationalist gunners saw looking down the slopes, across the town of Guadarrama, and beyond to Madrid. Around the bunker are the remains of trenches.
(7) Leave the bunker and walk some 50 meters north toward the fence. Keep the red and white communications mast on your left. There is a gap in between the fence and the rocks. The footpath GR10—which is marked with red, white, and green stripes—passes through this gap.
(8) Just beyond the gap in the fence is a stone-built Nationalist refuge; the extremities of the weather in the mountains meant that protection was essential.

Remains of a Nationalist refuge, Alto del León, with sweeping views of the sierra beyond. Exposure to sub-zero temperatures in the winter months could be as lethal as enemy fire. (James Ferguson)

(9) Follow the footpath GR10 with the red, white, and green stripes to the northeast—keep the fence to the right.

(10) The path passes a refuge with a barrel-shaped roof after 200 meters. To the left of this refuge is a maze of trenches, lookout posts, and gun emplacements which are well worth exploring.

(11) The GR10 continues north and drops down before rising again. On the upward slope are the remains of another fortification from the war. This is a good place to stop for a snack or water break and to take in the spectacular views before returning back along the GR10 to the Alto del León.

Valle de los Caídos

On 1 April 1940 a cavalcade of smart limousines swept out of Madrid. It was a pleasant afternoon, and General Franco was being escorted to the Sierra de Guadarrama. This excursion did not, however, offer the prospect of a bracing walk or some hunting (the dictator's favorite pastime). Franco was off to inspect the place where he would be buried.

The idea of building a grandiose mausoleum for himself had occurred to Franco soon after the Civil War ended. He and his wife went on several trips to the *sierra* looking for a suitable place for such a monument. As some people search for the dream location for their house, Franco wanted exactly the right spot to immortalize himself by building a huge basilica church to host his own tomb. The place he

General Franco
(Universidad de Alcalá)

finally settled on, called Cuelgamuros, was at the head of one of the most beautiful valleys in the *sierra* and ticked many of the right boxes. First, it was just a few kilometers from King Philip II's gigantic monastery-palace at El Escorial. Franco idolized the sixteenth-century Spanish monarch who sponsored the imperial expansion of the *conquistadores*, spread the Catholic faith, and upheld the supremacy of Spain. Franco sought to project a similar image; he repeatedly declared that the Civil War was a "crusade" to promote the integrity of traditional values and the sanctity of the Roman Catholic Church and to protect Spain from "foreign" ideas. Building a vast basilica just a few kilometers from King Philip's was a perfect fit in Franco's eyes and would link their names for eternity. Second, Cuelgamuros had been the scene of fierce fighting in the battle of the sierra. Franco wanted a place for his mausoleum which was associated with the war, and there was none better than the Sierra de Guadarrama. Third, the pharaonic structure Franco planned was to be so large that it would be clearly seen from Madrid. Henceforth, Cuelgamuros would be known as the Valle de los Caídos or Valley of the Fallen, with a huge church known as the basilica of the Holy Cross at the center.

The official decree announcing the project explained that its grandeur would be such as to "defy time and forgetfulness," and in this it achieved its objective: a visit to the valley certainly lingers in the memory. Covering almost 14 square kilometers, the dimensions of the Valle de los Caídos precinct are truly startling. Most of the Holy Cross church cannot actually be seen from the ground, as it is carved into the hillside—the central nave of the basilica is a tunnel, over 260 meters long and nearly 20 meters wide, excavated into the solid rock. (The original intention was to have a 9-meter wide nave until it became apparent that this induced a sensation of claustrophobia in most visitors.) The entrance is at one end of a giant esplanade, flanked by a crescent of gigantic pillars. Yet even these columns are dwarfed by the most dominant feature, a jaw-dropping giant cross 150 meters tall, which rises out of the huge outcrops of granite above the tomb. It is a measure of Franco's state of mind that he apparently wanted the complex to be even larger. It was only scaled down—if those are the right words—after objections from the Vatican that the basilica in the rock would be bigger than St. Peter's in Rome. Franco's tomb lies before the High Altar at the end of the basilica's nave. The gray stone slab is inscribed with a plain cross and Francisco Franco spelt out in capital letters, and every day there are fresh flowers on the tomb. Above ground, on the other side of the giant cross, is a Benedictine Abbey where the monks now pray for peace and the souls of the dead whilst a Requiem Mass is held in the basilica every 20 November to commemorate Franco's death.

The first occupant of the mausoleum was not, in fact, Franco but the Falangist leader José Antonio Primo de Rivera. José Antonio (as he is known to Spaniards) was the eldest son

The main door of the basilica leading to Franco's tomb. The cross is taller than the Statue of Liberty.
(Sebastian Dubiel/Wikimedia Commons)

of the dictator Miguel Primo de Rivera. In the spring of 1936 he was arrested for possessing unauthorized weapons and held by the Republican government—effectively as a political prisoner. He was taken to Valencia and executed by the Republic on 20 November 1936. José Antonio's Falange movement was an essential part of Franco's coalition during the Civil War and the early years of his dictatorship. Conveniently dead, the charismatic fascist leader posed no threat to Franco. He did, however, offer an iconic figure of martyrdom for Franco to manipulate and with which to placate the Falange. In the same way that Fidel Castro has used the image of Che Guevara, the wily Franco milked the legend of José Antonio for all it was worth. In 1940 a long, slow funeral cortege brought José Antonio's remains back from Valencia for a solemn mass in El Escorial. Waiting at the monastery were wreaths sent by both Hitler and Mussolini. The body was later reburied in the Valley of the Fallen when the colossal mausoleum was completed in 1959. There it remains to this day, alongside Franco, who was interred in the basilica when he died in 1975. On 20 November each year a solemn mass is still celebrated in the basilica, attended by hundreds of Falangist sympathizers.

The mausoleum was a costly distraction from much needed construction work in post-war Spain and was only made possible through the use of forced labor. By 1939 the Spanish economy had been shattered by the conflict, with shortages of everything—men, materials, and finance. In the 1940s, food was so scarce that many parts of the country were close to famine. National output did not recover to even pre-Civil War levels until 1956. The Franco regime had no problem, however, in identifying an important source of cheap labor for the mausoleum project: Republican prisoners. Under a series of "catch all" laws, Franco sought retribution for everything which happened in "the red zone" from 18 July 1936 until the "liberation." It was retrospective justice similar to the reparations demanded by the Allies from Germany at Versailles in 1919—but in this case one half of Spain would be paying the other. At one point, up to half a million prisoners were held and 100,000 organized into 121 labor battalions. All over Spain, those who had fought on the wrong side were put to work on civil construction schemes. Franco apparently believed that their "political crimes" could be "redeemed" by work, and prisoners toiled under the slogan *el trabajo enoblece* ("work enobles")—a chilling Iberian echo of the message above the gates of every Nazi concentration camp: *Arbeit Macht Frei* (Work Frees).

The extent to which the Valle de los Caídos was a forced labor camp and part of the overall system remains a topic of hot debate. Thousands of people worked on the site but not all were there on the same terms, and conditions changed over the years. Some men were skilled technicians and construction workers who worked voluntarily at the going rate. Others, especially at the start of the project, were undoubtedly political prisoners. Yet more, it seems, worked under duress for a few pesetas. The blacklisting of ex-Republicans after the war was common, and the consequences for them and their families dire. Working on the Valle de los Caídos, even on low pay and with harsh conditions, was one way out.

The Valle de los Caídos complex took more than two decades to complete. Franco took a detailed interest—planning, advising, and visiting—at every new phase. Professor Paul Preston quotes the observation that "the Valle de los Caídos was the closest Franco ever came to having a mistress." The cost—over a billion pesetas—was taken from the proceeds of the national lottery and from donations. In the cash-strapped Spanish economy of the 1940s and 1950s, where many still went hungry and uneducated, that alone was a high price to pay.

Half a century after the dictator's death, the Valle de los Caídos remains at the center of a conflict about how to record Spain's past. From Northern Ireland to South Africa, there have been different models of what is now called conflict resolution, aimed at healing the scars of war and civil conflict.

Little similar has been attempted in Spain. The official historic memory is asymmetrical, wholly skewed to honor the victors and muffle the vanquished, although the last socialist (PSOE) government (2004–2012) passed a *Ley de Memoria Histórica* (Historical Memory Law) to facilitate greater disclosure about the past. This legislation included an attempt to put the Valle de los Caídos on a new footing. The monument, which is owned and run on behalf of the state by the Spanish national heritage agency known as Patrimonio Nacional, was closed down for essential "repairs." Meanwhile, the government set up a commission of experts to examine the question of what should be done with the monument in the future. They came up with several recommendations about how to "de-politicize" the valley, including a new educational center to give an objective view of history, and the removal of the tombs of Franco and José Antonio so that they could be reburied in family plots. The report was shelved when the PSOE lost power in 2012. In the current political climate, it is more likely that bullfighting will be banned throughout Spain before anything radical happens to the Valle de los Caídos.

Directions to Valle de los Caídos

The monuments of the Valle de los Caídos are open from 10AM to 5PM (winter) and 10AM to 6PM (summer), and closed on Mondays. At the time of writing, the entrance fee for EU citizens in 2014 is €4, and non-EU citizens €9.

The Basilica of the Valle de los Caídos is 58 kilometers from Madrid. By car: From Madrid take the AP6 (A Coruña) highway, and then *salida* (exit) 47 direction El Escorial-Guadarrama. The entrance to the Valle de los Caídos is on the M600 road between San Lorenzo de El Escorial and Guadarrama. With large imposing gates set slightly off the road, it is opposite the junction of the M600 with the Calle Carlos Martínez, which leads to Villalba.

By bus: there is a regular bus service from Madrid

intercambiador (bus/Metro station) Moncloa to the main entrance of the Valle de los Caídos. The bus is no. 664 and goes to San Lorenzo de El Escorial via Guadarrama, with a stop outside the main entrance to the Valle de los Caídos. There is no shuttle bus service between the main entrance and the basilica—a distance of 6 kilometers. The walk down the valley, however, passes through some spectacular countryside with great views. There is a daily return bus service from the bus station in San Lorenzo de El Escorial to the basilica. The bus leaves at 3:15PM, goes to the Valle de los Caídos (including the basilica), and then returns to San Lorenzo de El Escorial.

THE MONASTERY OF EL ESCORIAL

San Lorenzo de El Escorial is a small town which owes it existence to the very large monastery in its center. The monastery was built by King Philip II (1527–98) and also doubled as his royal palace. This neatly combined the two things to which Phillip was devoted throughout his life: power and the Roman Catholic faith. The monastery-palace took more than three decades to complete, and when finished in 1584 it was one of the largest buildings in the world. The monastery alone covers 33,000 square meters, and also spawned a school and a university. There are more than 1,000 rooms, 88 staircases, 86 fountains, and several kilometers of corridors. The precinct was developed further as new buildings to house embassies, courtiers, and a miscellany of regal hangers-on.

El Escorial has been listed as a World Heritage Site by the United Nations. Even that accolade, however, does not do justice to the importance of the place in Spanish history and culture—or in the collective Castilian psyche. Sixteenth-century Spain was a global power to be reckoned with. Its imperial reach stretched from Holland in the north, through parts of Austro-Hungary and Italy, to the Caribbean and the Americas in the west. Perhaps the biggest disappointment in Phillip's life was his failure to rule England. He was briefly married to

The monastery palace of El Escorial
(Stephen A. Borish/Wikimedia Commons)

the English Queen Mary I and then sent his Armada on an unsuccessful mission to invade Britain in 1588. Nevertheless, sixteenth-century Spain was a first order global power, and El Escorial was at the epicenter of its vast empire. The monastery complex came to join together the golden age of Spain with the all-pervasive power of the Catholic Church.

Even though Spain's global power declined, El Escorial continued to exert a powerful hold on the Spanish mind into the twentieth century. The elegant town, with its beautiful setting, was a magnet for the well-to-do and a source of political gossip. The founder of the Spanish socialist PSOE Pablo Iglesias, for example, was frequently—and falsely—rumored by his enemies to have had "a chalet in El Escorial." The smear implied that he was somehow corrupt or bourgeois—and most likely both. The leftist President of the Second Republic, Manuel Azaña, really did live in the town, but was marked by the experience. He was sent to study there under the tutelage of the monastery's Augustinian monks. This led him into a complex relationship with the Catholic Church and was possibly at the root of his anti-clericalism. In the 1920s, Azaña published a novella which dealt with the sexual and intellectual awakening of an adolescent educated under a strict religious order. Setting it in El Escorial, Azaña called his book *El jardín de los frailes* (*The Monks' Garden*).

The monastery actually does have a famous Italianate garden called the Jardín de los Frailes: it has stunning views and is well worth a visit.

The Spanish political right forged a stronger bond than did Azaña with just about everything that El Escorial represented. In 1927 General Franco—already a rising star in the Spanish army—was tasked with founding a new national Military Academy. Franco pushed for the center to be sited in El Escorial but was overruled by the dictator of the time, Miguel Primo de Rivera, who insisted that the academy be established in the northern city of Zaragoza. Franco later commented ruefully that had the academy been in El Escorial (much closer to Madrid), he could have forestalled the abdication of King Alfonso XIII in 1931 and aborted the birth of the Second Republic.

Many on the far right never accepted the legitimacy of the Second Republic, and soon began to plot against it. El Escorial was again at the center of events. In the autumn of 1933 leaders of the fascist Falange and the monarchist Renovación Española met in San Lorenzo and reached what became known as the El Escorial Pact. In return for finance from wealthy monarchist backers, the Falangists agreed to support a future military uprising. It was an important step toward unifying the anti-Republican forces of the right and another step towards the Civil War. The far right also used El Escorial for more public events. In what Paul Preston describes as "a deliberately provocative anti-republican gesture," El Escorial was chosen as a backdrop for one of their biggest mass meetings a few months later. On 22 April 1934 some 20,000 young fascists gathered there to stage a Nazi-style rally. The threat of armed violence against the Republic hung heavily in the air, and the general mood was summed up in the speech of one reactionary deputy who raged that the government of "Jews, heretics, protestants, admirers of the French revolution, Freemasons, liberals, and Marxists" were "outside and against the Fatherland and are anti-Fatherland."

When the Civil War broke out in the summer of 1936, El

Escorial was rapidly engulfed by the conflict. San Lorenzo was one of the largest towns in the area, and the battle for control of the Sierra de Guadarrama was fought out along the heights immediately behind it. The town was held by the Republicans and coveted by the Nationalists—both sides fully recognized its symbolic and strategic importance. On 22 November 1936 a broadcast from the Nationalist-controlled Radio Burgos declared

> The Head of State, his *Excelentísimo Señor* General Franco, has indicated that the imminent capture of El Escorial and its monastery of San Lorenzo, the principal religious and historic center of Spain, will be the same as the conquest of the capital. In respect of Madrid the General does not consider it just to take the city by armed force and will thereby avoid the unnecessary spilling of blood.

This was, of course, pure bluster. The rebel attack on Madrid had by then failed (see Chapters 5 and 6). Nevertheless, the broadcast demonstrated the unique status of San Lorenzo de El Escorial. There was probably no other town in Spain that Franco was prepared to name as a surrogate for the real capital and so claim victory in the war, but in the event, the rebels were no more successful in taking El Escorial than they had been in Madrid. In December 1936 the Nationalists tried to cut the road linking the town with the capital. The attack failed, and El Escorial remained in Republican hands though all reference to San Lorenzo was dropped—the town became El Escorial de la Sierra for the duration of the war.

El Escorial became an increasingly important center for the Republican forces, and the buildings immediately around the monastery were pressed into use as offices, stores, and dormitories. The town itself was a safe haven for military supply, rest, and recuperation—Nationalist reverence for the unique monastery meant that it was relatively unscathed by shelling or aerial attack. El Escorial was also an important medical center, the main hospital down the hill toward the railway station in a religious seminary (the building has since been demolished). Although the conditions were at times described as "terrible," the patients were at least protected from attack because of their proximity to the monastery. The center served as the main field hospital for the wounded from the Guadarrama front, and in the summer of 1937 it was also requisitioned for use for the wounded from the Battle of Brunete. The mortally injured German-Jewish photographer Gerda Taro, for example, was taken to the hospital and died there of her wounds (see Chapter 8).

The most famous British patient here was Julian Bell. Born in Gordon Square, London, in 1908, his parents Vanessa and Clive were both artists who belonged to the fashionable Bloomsbury Group. Virginia Woolf was his aunt. After a conventional education (Quaker public school and Cambridge), he went to China in 1935 to become a Professor of English. When the war broke out in Spain, Bell decided that he must join the fight. He was not a communist, but had been deeply influenced by the Confucian creed that Right Thoughts are pointless unless they lead to Right Action (more prosaically expressed, perhaps, in the old dictum that "actions speak louder than words"). His mother and aunt tried desperately to stop him and called on several persuasive friends, including the novelist E. M Forster and poet Stephen Spender, to try to talk him out of the idea. Bell caved into the family pressure—but not completely. He agreed to join the medical service rather than fight as a volunteer, and left for Spain early in June 1937.

The following month, the Republic launched a huge offensive at Brunete, some 40 kilometers to the west of Madrid. Bell was in the thick of the fighting. Far from being in a safe occupation, frontline medics were among those most exposed: half the British Medical Unit were killed at Brunete, and Bell was among them. On 15 July his ambulance was destroyed by shell fire but three days later a replacement arrived. Bell was ferrying wounded from near a village called Villanueva de la Cañada to the hospital in El Escorial when his new ambulance was attacked by the German Luftwaffe. He took cover underneath the vehicle but was hit by a large piece of shrapnel. Triaged as a hopeless case when he first arrived at the hospital in El Escorial, the young ambulance driver was, incredibly, still conscious. "Well, I always wanted a mistress and a chance to go to war and now I have had both," he murmured. The British doctors quickly recognized Bell as one of their own medical team and did all they could to save him. One managed to extract his wallet and passport, which had been blown deep into the gaping chest wound, but part of his heart was exposed and nothing more could be done. He died a few hours later.

Fundraisers for the Spanish Medical Aid Committee, London
(Mesón El Cid)

The doctors in the El Escorial hospital were part of the Spanish Medical Aid Committee, an organization set up in London in July 1936 to channel medical support from the United Kingdom to the Republic. Peter Churchill, Winston's cousin, was a treasurer. During the course of the war the committee raised well over £50,000, sent out more than 70 ambulances, and supported medical staff working all over the Republican zone (not just with the International Brigades). Among the British doctors who tried to save Julian Bell in El Escorial, several went on to have distinguished careers in medicine. His friend Dr. Kenneth Sinclair-Loutit became a regional director in the World Health Organization. Dr. Archie Cochrane became a captain in the Royal Army Medical Corps and prisoner of war in World War II. He was appointed Professor at the Welsh National School of Medicine, where he founded a database of clinical trials called the UK Cochrane Centre, now based in Oxford. Dr. Reginald Saxton pioneered new techniques for organizing blood banks and administering transfusions on a battlefield. These innovations saved many lives in Spain and were taken up by the British army in World War II, and Saxton himself went on to serve with the British Army Transfusion Service in Burma.

In one sense, these doctors were lucky because they left Spain and, literally, lived to fight another day. The Spanish director of the hospital in El Escorial, Fernando Ortiz, was less fortunate. Along with colleagues—and many others—he was executed in a wave of reprisal killings by the victorious Nationalists.

The end of the resistance in Madrid signaled the end of the war in the *sierra* too. On 28 March 1939 rebel forces entered El Escorial. Many people were soon rounded up, and the Mayor of San Lorenzo de El Escorial, Vicente Carrizo, was amongst them. Vicente was a local, born in San Lorenzo in 1900. He began to study medicine, but when his father died the family ran out of money to support him. Vicente returned to San Lorenzo and became a teacher in the school, which was on the upper floor of what is now the town's market. In the early 1930s he involved himself in the civic life of San Lorenzo. He became a PSOE councilor, president of the local soccer club, and then mayor in 1932. These were years of frenetic social reform. Vicente kicked off projects for a new school, a new hospital, and an overhaul of the town's crumbling drainage system. A fluent French speaker, he escorted the French Prime Minister, Édouard Herriot, while on an official visit to the monastery in 1932.

All that stopped abruptly when the right won the national elections in 1934. Like so many others, Vicente was suspended from public office and only reinstated as mayor when the left won the elections of February 1936. Surviving records speak of Vicente's humanity during the conflict. Many in Madrid's wealthy bourgeoisie had second homes around San Lorenzo where they spent the summer—the fresh mountain air is still infinitely preferable to the stifling heat of the city in July and August. San Lorenzo de El Escorial remained loyal to the Republic when the war broke out in July 1936, leaving several of its well-heeled summer residents on the wrong side of the line and open to reprisals. Vicente signed safe conduct passes and organized a special train to get them to the Nationalist zone. Later in the year, however, Spain descended into a vortex of ugly reprisals. Scores or monks from the monastery of El Escorial were among the victims of the Republican-orchestrated massacre at Paracuellos (see Chapter 4).

By mid-March 1939 it was clear that the Nationalists were about to lose the war. Vicente, a well-known mayor of one of the most recognizable frontline towns, was offered safe passage to Mexico, but he refused. His wife told him, "you are a good man and have nothing to fear." She was wrong.

Vicente met the commanding officer of the occupying forces in the town hall with his characteristic grace. The two, it seems, even exchanged civil words as he handed over the mayor's ceremonial pistol and seals of office. Yet within days Vicente was denounced along with scores more of the town's citizens and imprisoned. He was put on trial for his life, before a military tribunal which held its sessions in the small casino of San Lorenzo. Vicente declined a lawyer and conducted his own defense with some success, insofar as he avoided a death sentence. He was, however, given a jail sentence of thirty years. Back in prison he wrote comforting letters to his three young children in which he tried to shield them from the dreadful truth. He fantasized about life in jail and told them, "every night I have a vision that mummy comes to see me dressed as a fairy!" There was to be no happy ending to this tale. The authorities were infuriated with the "lenient" sentence handed down to Vicente and put him on trial again, on the same charges. He and his wife desperately tried to pull strings with anyone of influence they knew in the new regime, but it was to no avail, and this time Vicente was sentenced to death. General Franco would often review and sign off the capital sentences while taking his post-lunch coffee. Perhaps Vicente's name was one of those who passed through the caudillo's hands. If so, Franco showed no mercy, and the former Mayor of San Lorenzo de El Escorial was executed on 17 November 1939.

Vicente Carrizo was just one of some 20,000 people who were officially eliminated in the years of reprisals following Franco's victory in March 1939. On an official visit to Madrid in 1940, even the top Nazi Heinrich Himmler expressed his surprise at the scale of the reprisals. The exact numbers may never be known, but the repression carried out by the Franco regime was on an industrial scale and designed to eliminate, in the words General Mola, "without scruple or hesitation those who do not think as we do."

New research is now being undertaken by local groups all over Spain about killings which took place during and after the war. In San Lorenzo de El Escorial, scores of people were executed and then buried in the tranquil local parish cemetery, but not with any dignity. The victims lie in a mass grave under the main patio so that even today visitors must walk over them when entering and leaving. It is only recently that relatives have been able to put up a small memorial in one corner which records their names and reads: "They could not achieve it but are not alone because we are here, they did not lose everything because we are here, they did not fight in vain because we are here, we are the memory of their future. Liberty - Equality - Fraternity."

Hundreds of thousands of other Republicans fled over the border to France, where they were unwelcome and held in camps by the French authorities. Past power and privilege counted for nothing. Largo Caballero, who as Prime Minister of the Republic boosted the moral of the militiamen with his visit to the Sierra de Guadarrama in the summer of 1936, fled to France. He was arrested by the Gestapo in 1940 and sent to Dachau concentration camp outside Munich. He died, broken, in 1946. Manuel Azaña, the student in El Escorial who went on to become President of the Second Republic, fled over the Pyrenees, but he was hounded through France by Franco's spies and the Gestapo. His health shattered, Azaña died in a small hotel room in Montauban near Toulouse in 1940. Ironically, the street outside the hotel has been renamed Rue de la Résistance, with a plaque bearing the names of all the townsfolk who were executed for resisting the Nazis.

In San Lorenzo de El Escorial, however, there is next to nothing to mark the presence in the town of the president, the mayor, the hospital director, volunteers like Julian Bell, or, indeed, anyone else who died fighting much the same thing as the citizens of Montauban.

Visiting El Escorial

There is a regular return bus service from Madrid *intercambiador* (bus/Metro station) Moncloa. Buses to San Lorenzo de El Escorial are the 661 via Galapagar or the 664 via Guadarrama. The journey time is the same on both routes: around 45 minutes.

The monastery is open from 10AM to 5PM (winter) and 10AM to 6PM (summer), and closed on Mondays. At the time of writing, the entrance fee is €10 and €5 for students and pensioners. On Wednesday and Thursday afternoons, entrance is free to EU citizens.

Entry to the Jardín de los Frailes is free. Facing the main entrance to the monastery, the entrance is on the right underneath the arched walkway over the road.

The covered market is on the corner of Calle del Rey and Calle de las Pozas. The Casino de San Lorenzo de El Escorial is now a rather sleazy bar: 36 Calle del Rey.

The Cementerio Parroquial (parish cemetery) is in the Paseo Miguel de Unamuno (no number). The political prisoners were held in the convent in the nearby 2 Plaza de Santa Teresa, before being executed.

The Jardín de los Frailes, El Escorial (Juan Carlos Santamaria/ Wikimedia Commons)

8

THE BATTLE OF BRUNETE: IF NOT HERE, THEN WHERE?

"The army in Madrid is the best and... has all the available aircraft and a mass of artillery. If we cannot succeed with our forces here then we will not be able to manage it anywhere."

Diary entry of Manuel Azaña, President of the Second Republic, July 1937

"Over Brunete came the sound
of black wings crawling up the sky;
the soldier crouched against the ground
with straining limbs until they went by.
He heard the bombs sing down the air,
He felt them land, and everywhere
The earth in an advancing line rose up.
The soldier said 'this time'.
This time he laughed at what he said,
and stretched his body to the heat;
the sun alone was overhead
and warmed the terror out of it.

Now when the thin December gleam
is driven off the sky by snow
and breath hangs in the air like steam,
the soldier on the plain below
hears the familiar song of hate

and stoops behind the parapet.
When the black wings have passed beyond
He pulls his blanket closer round
grins at the younger man, who tries
to catch the courage from his eyes.
'We'll bring them all down by and by
and then' he says 'they'll never come.'
The young man, looking at the sky,
sees only white wings of the storm."

Miles Tomalin, volunteer, for *Liberty* magazine, no. 28, published in Madrid, 27 December 1937

By the summer of 1937, the Civil War in Spain had dragged on for almost a year and the siege of Madrid was into its ninth month. There had been no decisive breakthrough nor end in sight. One of the few sure things was the "internationalization" of the conflict and the build-up of foreign involvement. General Franco was by now heavily dependent on Hitler and Mussolini for war materiel, while the Republic was deeply in hock to the Soviet Union.

Republican commanders sought to break the deadlock by mobilizing for a massive offensive on the Nationalist line just outside Madrid. The attack, which became known as the Battle of Brunete, was expected to be a decisive strike against the rebels and to turn the war against Franco. But the assault quickly lost momentum. The two armies slogged it out for more than three weeks on the bare Castilian plain under the scorching summer sun. The battle turned into one of the bloodiest engagements of the war and, of the estimated 150,000 men involved, around a third were killed or wounded. Once again the International Brigades were in the thick of the action—and once again they suffered appalling losses.

Perhaps the most notable foreign casualty, however, was not a combatant but a witness to the carnage. Gerda Taro was a 26-year-old photographer who had been forced into exile from her native Germany when the Nazis came to power. Armed only with impetuous courage and a Leica camera, she captured some of the most moving images of the conflict. After her, war photography would never be the same again: she literally changed the way people saw the world.

This chapter and its tour follow in the footsteps of Taro to find out more about this crucial offensive and why it ended in failure for the Republic.

In the spring of 1937 the map of Spain looked like a half mounted jigsaw, with some areas held by the Nationalists, others by the Republicans. The war was being fought along several fronts simultaneously and going on much longer than anyone had expected. Gradually, however, the Nationalists were gaining the upper hand: while they had failed to score the expected quick victories in Madrid or Barcelona, the rebel forces were whittling down the Republic everywhere. Loyalist enclaves in the north of Spain were under particular pressure. In April 1937 German aircraft bombed the Basque town of Guernica into history and then seized the region's main port, Bilbao. The next target on the Nationalist list was the coastal city of Santander.

Republicans commanders wanted to relieve pressure on the beleaguered loyalists in the northern sector. In the late spring of 1937 they and their Russian advisors planned a major attack to break the Nationalist line just outside Madrid. The attack was to be a pincer movement, thrusting down from the north and up from the south. This would cut the Nationalist supply line from the west of Spain and leave the rebel forces besieging the capital surrounded.

With one blow the offensive would change the course of the war. The siege of Madrid, now in its ninth month, would be broken. Pressure would be taken off the beleaguered Republican forces in the north of the country. And Stalin, whose enthusiasm for the war was beginning to cool by this time, would be assured that the Republic was still up for a fight. Indeed, some government ministers thought that the offensive might actually broaden support: a decisive victory, they said, might finally persuade countries like Britain and France to get off the diplomatic fence and at last come to their aid.

Republican commanders had good reason to be optimistic that their plan would work. A single "popular army" was being forged from the ragbag of militia and regular units, and this was to be its first major offensive. The focal point of the initial attack was a sleepy *pueblo* 35 kilometers to the west of the capital called Brunete, an unassuming backwater where people scratched a living from the arid Castilian plain. The Battle of Brunete lasted for three weeks, from 5 to 27 July 1937, and there were three distinct phases. The first, between 6 and 11 July, went well for the Republicans, and they gained some 160 square kilometers of Nationalist territory. The second, between 11 and 17 July, saw stiff Nationalist resistance and a stalemate between the two forces. During the third phase, between 18 and 26 July, Nationalist counterattacks regained some lost ground and led to a war of attrition along the front which lasted until the end of the war.

Estimates vary, but around 150,000 men were involved in the fighting. One participant claimed that the Republicans had 150 planes, 128 tanks, and 136 pieces of artillery, and that the Nationalists had three times more. That may well be an exaggeration and exact numbers will never be known. What all sides agree on, however, is that it was certainly one of the bloodiest battles of the war. The rumble of artillery fire was heard in Madrid and the huge, billowing clouds of smoke and dust produced by the battle was easily visible from the city. At times the carnage was equal to that of the Western Front in World War I: somewhere between 40,000 and 50,000 men were killed, wounded, or missing. And, as in Belgium, the weather marked the course of this battle—not the rain and mud of Flanders, of course, but the searing heat of the midsummer sun—the battle raged throughout most of July in temperatures well over 40°C.

The offensive was planned with the utmost secrecy and this was helped by intelligence failures on all sides. The British journalist Henry Buckley said that he found out about the "surprise attack" weeks before it happened while hanging around the bars of Valencia (more than 350 kilometers from Madrid) and picking up gossip. "The strange thing was," wrote Buckley, "that it *did* actually seem to surprise the nationalists." The attack certainly caught General Franco on the hop. He had just set off for the northern front where he fully expected to see for himself the fall of Santander when the news of the offensive came through: some 80,000 Republican troops had smashed a 12-kilometer hole in the Nationalist line and were surging toward Madrid. Franco's car turned back immediately and his chief of staff, traveling with him, recalled "the time when I saw Franco most worried... was without a doubt during the reds' attack on the Madrid front at Brunete."

Republican planning for the offensive had in fact been going on for weeks. Entire divisions moved into the sector west of Madrid and then up to their jumping off points. Great care was taken to avoid being observed. Entire companies marched at night or were transported in trucks with covered headlights. Then they waited, camouflaged among the trees and olive groves. The charismatic communist leader Dolores Ibarruri (La Pasionaria) was among the Republican leaders who toured the battalions to raise morale: one soldier said that it was only when he saw her that it dawned on him that "something really serious was about to start." A Russian advisor wrote of how he spent 4 July observing Brunete and the Nationalist lines from one of the hills across the plain. Around him the soldiers checked, rechecked, and checked again their guns, ammunition, and equipment. (1)

During the night of 5/6 July, the Republican vanguard moved closer to the Nationalist line, led by pathfinders who had been specially trained to guide in the dark using just a compass. The midsummer sun on the plain of Madrid does not set until getting on for 10PM, and even then the temperature scarcely dipped below 30°C. According to one combatant, the sultry night air was "heavy and sticky, difficult to breathe." The standard kit of thick uniforms and heavy boots simply added to the discomfort.

Phase 1 of the Republicans' strategy required troops to push south along a front some 12 kilometers across and quickly seize three villages. The first was Brunete itself, at the spearhead of the offensive. The second was called Quijorna, on the right flank, and the third Villanueva de la Cañada, on the left flank. Once these villages were captured, a new line could be consolidated, allowing the Republican troops to push on further south and encircle the Nationalist army besieging Madrid. That, at least, was the plan. But the offensive stalled and two of the three villages, Quijorna and Villanueva de la Cañada, did not fall as anticipated. As the advance faltered and Republican losses rose, their quick victory did not happen and the open plain around Madrid became hell on earth. (2)

BRUNETE

The offensive had got off to a good start. Although Brunete was the objective furthest from the Republican lines it was easily taken on 6 July. (3) The assault on the village was carried out by the Republican 5th Regiment, led by the 31-year-old communist commander Enrique Líster. The column set off from near the village of Valdemorillo and marched the 12 kilometers south in silence through the dead of night. One soldier described the tension of the advance.

> We moved quickly through the night... like a chain of human ants threading its way down from the low foothills of the sierra along the dry paths that led to

> Brunete... The night was hot. My shirt was soaked with sweat and stuck to my ribs... We left the firm ground of the cattle trail and started to walk over dry stubble. The sound of people panting and the crunch of boots under straw hung in the air. Then an order ran down the column from front to back "Silence! We are crossing enemy lines."

The column reached the outskirts of Brunete just before dawn. The village had been fortified but the small band of rebel troops stationed there was quickly overcome, and by the end of the day Brunete was in Republican hands. Líster's men were jubilant at having rapidly completed their part of the operation with few losses and were ready to continue moving south toward the next objectives, the villages of Sevilla la Nueva and Navalcarnero, just a few kilometers further to the south of Brunete. But Líster hesitated. He was in danger of advancing too far too fast, leaving his flanks and rear exposed. Without support, there was a real possibility of a Nationalist counterattack encircling his men and leaving them stranded. So instead of pushing on, Líster ordered his men to dig in just south of Brunete and hold the position until reinforcements arrived. (4, 5)

Whether Líster made the right decision is a debate that goes on to this day. Some argue that he should have exploited the element of surprise and capitalized on the gain. Had they pushed on, his men would have made a decisive dent in the Nationalist line, leaving a second wave of Republican forces to mop up the resistance. Others argue that Líster was justified in his caution, that the chances of being surrounded were just too great. Whatever might have been, Líster decided to hold his men at Brunete and wait. It was a decision which saved the day for the rebels. Entire divisions were rapidly drafted to reinforce the Nationalist line between Brunete and Quijorna, making a Republican breakthrough towards the southwest almost impossible.

If the initial attack on Brunete was a success, how did the offensive go so badly wrong? For a start, the attack from south to north simply never got off the ground, so the pincer movement never took place. This could have been overcome had the momentum of the push from north to south been maintained, but it was not. On the third day, defense minister Indalecio Prieto reported to President Manuel Azaña that "the operations are going well although they are desperately slow." The misanthropic president was less sure. "From then on," recorded Azaña in his diary, "I thought things would turn out badly: slowness, sterility of surprise, wasted opportunities, failure. What are we going to do?"

The two main problems were the delays in securing the villages of Quijorna and Villanueva de la Cañada, on the right and left flank of the attack. Nationalist troops put up doughty resistance around both the villages, and neither fell as planned on 6 July.

Quijorna

In July 1937 Quijorna was a small village of 500 inhabitants. (6) It was defended by just two companies of Falangists and, according to the Republican operational plan, storming the village before dawn on 6 July should have taken just a few hours. In the event, it took three days. The initial attack failed and following that almost nothing went according to plan. It was decided to try and shell the village into submission, but as the tanks and artillery moved up toward Quijorna they became jammed in a bottleneck. It was daybreak before the attack started and by then, with the surrounding confusion and in the clear light of day, the Nationalists were easily able to repel this attack too.

Confusion and delays were compounded by elementary errors. The Republicans partially surrounded—but failed to seal off—roads into Quijorna. During the night of 6–7 July an entire battalion of fresh Nationalist troops managed to slip into the village to reinforce the defense. As a consequence, when the

A Russian T-26 tank outside Brunete (Ministerio de Educación, Cultura y Deporte, Archivo General de la Administración [Archivo Rojo])

Republicans renewed their attacked the following day, they had to overcome a force which was even stronger than it had been the night before.

Frustrated by failure, the Republican High Command doubled the number of battalions assigned to take Quijorna from two to four. The following day (8 July), tanks almost reached the village but they were not supported by infantry, which had been held back by heavy fire. One Republican combatant recalled the fighting throughout the afternoon and evening around the church, which (rebuilt) is still there today on the high ground in the center of the village. "Our lot attacked like savages whilst theirs held out among the ruins of the houses and in the church tower, which was still standing, [from where] the Moroccans kept up a ceaseless barrage of fire..."

Artur London, a 22-year-old Czech volunteer with the International Brigades, remembered that a group of Moroccan soldiers held out in the cemetery behind a solid stone wall. Despite repeated attempts, the Republican infantry were held back by a "hellish fire"; armed with ever reliable Mauser rifles, the Moroccans were expert marksmen. Eventually, after more shelling, "troops advanced close enough to start hurling grenades. Tombs flew into the air and the disinterred skeletons got mixed up with more recent corpses" as the Republicans finally overcame the resistance. During the early hours of 9 July they eventually took control of the village and all the ground down to the river. But "sun up was a horrible spectacle. We spent all day getting the wounded out. There were a large number of dead and the olive grove was shredded." Incidentally, London survived not only this scrape with death but many more: he went on to lead a unit of the French Resistance, was interned in a Nazi concentration camp, and, by the skin of his teeth, survived a show trial in his native Czechoslovakia after he became deputy foreign minister. (7)

Blame for the failure to take Quijorna as planned was pinned on the communist commander, Valentín González. Recriminations flew and a damaging rift developed within the communist leadership which never healed. Better known as *El Campesino* (see Chapter 7) González had actually worked—from the age of eight—not on the land but in the mines of Andalucia. He became active in the communist trade union and was given command of troops at various battles during the war. In 1939 he escaped to the USSR, but it was a decision he subsequently regretted because after criticizing Stalin he was sent to a Siberian labor camp. He managed to escape during an earthquake, and made his way to Iran. For the next two decades González wandered in exile, and only returned to Madrid following the death of Franco. He died in 1983 in the city he fought so hard to defend.

The journalist Geoffrey Cox recorded that of all the Republican leaders, "the most vivid personality was the huge, dark-bearded figure of González. Still in his thirties, looking half Moor, half Cossack, he was the old guerrilla fighter of Spain in a modern setting." Another combatant recalled that he certainly engendered fear—as much on his own side as among the enemy. "The guy was a fiend although you can't deny he was brave. People were really afraid of him. Anyone who tried to chicken out was shot and if he was around he would finish them off with his white mother of pearl pistol." Whoever was responsible for the failure at Quijorna—victory has many parents, but defeat is an orphan—the delay severely hobbled the Republican attack. This was bad enough, but it was compounded by problems on the other side of the Republican line where nothing was going according to plan.

VILLANUEVA DE LA CAÑADA

On the left flank of the Republican offensive, the village of Villanueva de la Cañada was another crucial target. (8) The only road south—critical for the movement of munitions, food, and water—passed through Villanueva, and taking the village was essential to secure the Republican supply line before the offensive could continue. But, as with Quijorna, the Republican assault on Villanueva was botched, and in the end it took nearly 24 hours to occupy the tiny village. Problems could have been anticipated: even from a distance with binoculars, Republican reconnaissance scouts had reported on the concrete and barbed wire fortifications which surrounded Villanueva de la Cañada, where a garrison of 800 well armed Falangists was stationed. At 5:30AM on 6 July an artillery barrage rocked the village for an hour, followed by two waves of aerial bombing. The Republicans hoped that this would soften up the defenses. To a 16-year-old Falangist stationed five kilometers away, the attack did indeed look ferocious: "the ground was shaking… flames extended along the horizon. It was a brilliant spectacle… as I imagined hell to be."

Dawn broke and Republican infantry charged in from the north, but the attack failed. As the men approached within

100 meters of the barbed wire and trenches, they were mown down from machine gun positions which had survived the bombardment intact. The bombing had reduced the buildings of the village to rubble but left the surrounding defenses largely unscathed. At 11AM the Republicans launched a second assault, but once again a lack of coordination led directly to failure. The village was shelled by artillery and tanks but, inexplicably, there was a long delay before the infantry were sent in. This break gave the Nationalists plenty of time to emerge from their dugouts, reorganize, and repel the assault when it came.

Republican chiefs of staff were perplexed by the repeated setbacks—"dumbfounded" was the word used by one observer who noted that "the Divisional chiefs did not know what to do." Some fumed impotently at the delay, while General Miaja bawled an order to "take Cañada at all costs and if the infantry will not go forward place a battery of guns behind our own troops and make them." In fact, the battlefield around the village was already strewn with corpses, while burning tanks stood immobilized on the road spewing out thick black smoke. A third assault was launched in the early afternoon: the village church, which was being used as a field hospital, caved in during the preliminary shelling and 100 wounded were killed. But still the garrison could not be dislodged.

The British Battalion of the XV International Brigade, led by Jarama veterans Fred Copeman and Bill Meredith, had expected to bypass the village and push on to the high ground beyond (called the Monte Romanillos, or Romanillos Heights). But the stubborn Nationalist resistance led to a change of plan and the British found themselves thrown into the thick of the fight to take Villanueva. Volunteer Frank Graham recalled advancing along the dirt road which led from the village to El Escorial "over the rough, dry plain. The village was defended with pillboxes and gun emplacements" while "the church tower, which dominated the plain, was fortified and held several machine guns."

American volunteer Harry Fisher from the International Brigades elaborated on the problem:

> We were in a cornfield outside the village. The ground was hard and dry. The fascists firing the machine guns were lodged up in the bell tower of the church from where they had a clear view over the surrounding country... We were like sitting ducks because although the corn stems were high enough to hide us they moved with any movement and this attracted the enemy machine guns. At one point I tried to change position so that I could grip my rifle more firmly but the movement attracted the fire in my direction. The fire went on for hours without a break. We waited and waited trapped in the cornfield incapable of moving. The wounded were groaning and begging for water. As time went on I too started to have a terrible thirst—the need for water was so strong that it canceled out any other thought or feeling.

And so another assault fizzled out. The British Battalion now decided to skirt around the back of the village and try a different approach. They cut the road leading south to Brunete and came in close to Villanueva. But "it was clear that we would have to wait until dusk" before making a final assault, wrote Frank Graham, and this meant waiting in the heat of the July sun where "the fields in the rear of Villanueva were flat with no ditches or any cover. The men were exhausted with extreme heat and lack of water. The sun beat down for hour after hour and many passed out with heat stroke." (9)

In the early evening, a fourth attempt was made to take the village from all sides. Reinforcements had now moved up to take part but the Republicans were still not able to get within more than 100 or 200 meters of the Nationalist trenches. Finally, it was decided to wait until nightfall for the fifth attempt. Yet if the Republicans were desperate to get into the village, the

Nationalist garrison was equally desperate to get out or get help. Their casualties had been heavy—of the 1,000 who started the day, just 200 were still able to fight, and their ammunition was all but spent. All communication with the surrounded village had been cut. The Nationalist commander decided to try to get some men out, who could attempt to break through the line.

Night fell and a small group of pathetic refugees, mainly women and children, left the village. "Don't fire!" someone shouted, "there are children coming out of the village." Volunteer Jack Roberts recalled, "believing them to be refugees we called them forward. Some of us were now standing, some walking to meet and welcome them." The British had, of course, "fallen for an old trick." Mixed in with the civilians were Falangists. "The fascists who had been driving this group of old men, women, and children as cover started throwing hand-grenades in our midst. For a few minutes pandemonium reigned. It was hard to distinguish friend from foe." Decades after the event, Roberts said he could still hear the crash of grenades, the barking of guns, and the shrieks of the women and children.

The British then charged forward and stormed the village. "We lighted the streets with the red light of bursting grenades as we drove the fascists before us into the center of the town." Unbeknown to the British, the Balkan Dimitrov Battalion of the International Brigade and Spanish troops were attacking from the other end of the village. The two sides met near the middle—and nearly opened fire on each other. As the Republicans mopped up street by street ("we succoured the wounded no matter whether they were ours or the enemy") an incident occurred which embittered the British for years afterwards. "A wounded man cried out. Bill Meredith... bent down to attend to the cry for help. For answer he got a bullet through the heart from the wounded fascist." According to some reports, Fred Copeman now held back the furious volunteers to avoid reprisals. Others suggest that they continued to mop up, but now with little regard for the Geneva Conventions.

By midnight the village was secured and more than 100 Falangists were imprisoned in a local barn. More importantly still for the exhausted Republican troops, trucks arrived with food and—crucially—water. Little remained of the night for rest and recuperation, and when dawn broke on 7 July the men were sickened by what they saw. Fred Thomas, a volunteer with the British anti-tank battery, described how "the road by the village was lined with 40 dead bodies. Those that were pulled out from the tanks looked the worst." In the village, hundreds of dead lay under the rubble. Another volunteer recalled the stench of the corpses in the warm air with the buzzing of "flies, flies, and more flies."

If the immediate cost of taking Villanueva de la Cañada was great, the damage inflicted on the Republican offensive was irretrievable, and it never recovered the lost momentum. Like Quijorna, what looked like a simple operation on the map had turned into a fiasco. Hundreds were dead and wounded. It had taken a day longer than planned. Troops had been diverted to assist in the assault on the village and valuable time lost. According to the battle plan, Republican forces should already have advanced toward a small village called Boadilla del Monte on the outskirts of Madrid. The delay meant that this was about to be the next catastrophe.

MOSQUITO CREST, CASTILLO DE VILLAFRANCA, AND ROMILLOS HEIGHTS

On 6–7 July a rapid, direct Republican assault on the Nationalist garrison at Boadilla del Monte might well have succeeded. When British volunteer Frank Graham went scouting the area between the Guadarrama river and the outskirts of Boadilla on horseback, he reported that the Nationalists were nowhere to be seen. But over the next couple of days this position changed with deadly consequences. There was no immediate assault on Boadilla—just more setbacks. While Republican forces regrouped after the fiasco at Villanueva de la Cañada, the Nationalists seized the chance to strengthen their line. It was not until 9 July that the Republicans began to march on Boadilla, and by this time their offensive had been rolling on for three days. Any element of surprise had been lost. Fresh divisions of Nationalist troops from the north of Spain were streaming in to reinforce the Brunete front along the line. Outside Boadilla, the rebels were now well dug in, ready, and waiting for the Republicans' next move.

The XV International Brigade, which included the American and British Battalions, was among those designated to take Boadilla del Monte. The village was to the southeast of Villanueva de la Cañada, on the other side of the Guadarrama river beyond some low hills. Crossing the river did not present a problem—it had all but dried up in the heat—but conquering the hills, the Monte de Romillos, was a far more hazardous proposition. International Brigade volunteers nicknamed one particular hill "Mosquito Crest" because it buzzed perpetually with the sound of flying bullets. Along with Suicide Hill in the Jarama valley and Hill 466 on the River Ebro, Mosquito Crest entered into the annals of International Brigade history as a death trap. (10)

The battle for Mosquito Crest started on 9 July and went on for ten bloody days. Storming the hill was always going to be a formidable task; in the words of one Nationalist combatant, the hill was "like a wall which had been deliberately put there to defend the village [Boadilla] against attack from this direction. It was really clear in practice. The reds [republicans], to attack us, were exposed during an advance of at least two kilometers up sharply rising ground. We, meanwhile, were beautifully positioned. The only problem was that the ground was covered with bits of woodland and thick bushes which were easy to hide under. The only way to have got us, though, would have been to go round the hills from the south..." Such a maneuver, however, would have stretched the Republican forces to breaking point.

From the other side of the crest, a British volunteer with the International Brigades described the scene as they pushed east up the rising ground toward Boadilla del Monte. "On 9 July under heavy shellfire we made an advance of nearly two miles to within several hundred yards of the main fascist position. Our line was shaped like a spearhead with our position at the point. The fascists held the high ground, their fire sweeping our line of communications and our fighting positions." As happened so often during the Battle of Brunete, supply lines broke down so that fighting troops were left without food or precious water. "Down from our positions into the valley and up the hillside behind us ran the line of communications. It was raked night and day by snipers, machine guns, artillery, and aviation... For hours on end we crouched hugging the ground, face down, while the drone of Italian and German bombers filled the air and the very hillside rocked as one after another they loosed their cargo of death." The volunteer commented ruefully that with support on either flank their position would have been an ideal point from which to launch a final assault on Mosquito Crest. But that support never came.

Instead, the volunteers of the International Brigades were left on the exposed hillside for well over a week. The withering heat, constant machine gun fire, and ever increasing air attacks took their toll on morale. Lincoln Battalion volunteer Harry Malofsky wrote back home: "comrades, don't for a minute think that this war is 'glorious.' Every inch of the way is blood and sweat. The sun is terribly hot and many days we had to go without food and water because our trucks were bombed. The hardest part is seeing the comrades we knew and loved falling by our side."

Day after day futile attempts were made to dislodge the Nationalists from their well dug-in positions at the top of the crest, but the only progress made was in the casualty rate. The mauling of the five International Brigades at Brunete was intense. Of the 13,353 who started the battle a third (4,239) were killed, lost, or wounded. The XV Brigade was worst hit. Of the 2,144 men who went into action 1,259—a staggering 58 percent of the total—were casualties. And the battalion of the XV Brigade worst hit was the British. Of the 331 who went into battle, just 42 were in a condition to fight on three weeks later.

Not surprisingly, maintaining morale became a battle in itself, and the commander of the Lincolns, Steve Nelson, described the scene late one evening as he tried to cajole the weary, dispirited volunteers into one more attack. Climbing onto a rock, he could not see their faces in the dark but heard their murmuring as he spoke. When he finished there was silence. Finally, a voice said, "for God's sake, Steve, you're not telling us that we have to go back!" And yet that is exactly what they did. Other methods of persuasion were less subtle: the shattered remnants of the British Battalion only agreed to fight on after it was made clear to them that their commanding officer would be executed if they did not.

Not that it mattered much for the officers whether the bullets came from in front or behind. *The Book of the XV Brigade*, published by the volunteers themselves in 1938 to record their experiences in Spain, records dryly that "the British Battalion lost most of its leaders" in the three weeks at Brunete. Without doubt the most heartfelt loss was that of Major George Nathan, Chief of Staff of the XV International Brigade, who was hit in the back by shrapnel and killed on 16 July.

A Jewish Londoner, Nathan had served as a private on the Western Front during World War I. After demobilization, he stayed in the army where his innate intelligence and leadership skills propelled him up through the ranks and into a commission. His political views crystallized after a confrontation in the officers' mess during the General Strike of 1926. Troops were issued with rounds of live ammunition and officers told to order their use against the strikers if necessary. When Nathan expressed his horror, a senior officer rounded on him: "I think that you should not forget that, wherever you came from, now you are one of us. You must know that you have been very lucky. If you do not appreciate this, you had better get back as soon as possible to wherever you came from."

Nathan was taken to the hospital in El Escorial but died within hours. His loss was a bigger blow to the morale of the XV Brigade—and the British Battalion in particular—than any other. As one of the earliest volunteers to arrive in Spain, he fought with immense courage at the Battle of Jarama in February. South African volunteer Jason Gurney remembered him as "the only personality serving with the International Brigades who (was) an authentic hero figure, with a mythology of his own. A number of individuals of all nations behaved magnificently but none of them had the essential larger-than-life quality that distinguished George Nathan." Another recalled that he was "spiffy and regimented... during lulls in the battle he entertained visitors to lunch under shaded oak trees, offering them sliced tomato salad and fruit jam, served on a table carefully laid by his batman, whom he kissed and fondled openly." It was said that Nathan was gay. This, and his refusal to join the Communist Party, would normally have seen him airbrushed out of the Soviet records, but even the Russian advisor's report to Moscow spoke admiringly of Nathan's "cool arrogance under fire."

By July 1937 the officers and men of the XV International Brigade had seen a lot of killing, but when Nathan's body was returned to the battlefield of Brunete many wept openly at his improvised funeral. His body was buried among the native evergreen oak trees which line the banks of the River Aulencia, although it is no longer known exactly where.

Nathan's death came hard on the heels of another which had hit the American Lincoln Battalion—that of Oliver Law, from Chicago. Law was chief of their machine gun company and had been given the command because of his "coolness under fire," but there was something else which also marked him out. He was a black American. A visiting journalist once asked him why he was in Spain. "We came here to wipe out Fascists," he replied. "By doing it here in Spain maybe we'll stop Fascism in the United States too, without a great battle there. The people of Spain have the same aim as the Negro people—we are both fighting for our national independence."

According to one eye witness quoted in *The Book of the XV Brigade*, "Law died at the head of his troops, taking the machine gun company into a new position—a leader to the last." His comrade Harry Fisher was with Law and saw what happened. On the morning of 9 July, the Lincolns came under sustained and heavy fire as they surged up Mosquito Crest. Most took cover but Law stayed standing, completely exposed to the fire, urging them on. "The bullets seemed to have him as their only target," said Fisher. Someone shouted at Law to get down, but it was too late. The captain doubled up, hit in the stomach. Law began to crawl down the dust and the scrub of the hillside. The others dragged him into the cover of their position. "It's not serious," he told them, "I'll be back in a few days." An hour later he was dead. The Lincons buried their captain near the spot where he fell on the slopes of Mosquito Crest. Above the grave they erected a piece of wood with the inscription: "Here lies Oliver Law the first American negro to command white Americans in battle." His remains must still be there today, but the precise location has been lost with time. The wooden memorial has long since disappeared.

On 10–11 July the XII International Brigade finally took the village of Villanueva del Pardillo on the Republican left flank (towards the east), but could not make any significant progress. They crossed the Guadarrama river and briefly held the Castillo de Villafranca, a magnificent castle which had dominated the surrounding countryside since it was first constructed in the Middle Ages. Crack troops soon arrived from the northern front, however, to assist the Nationalist forces; savage fighting took place around the old castle, which was shelled incessantly,

A Republican machine gun crew defending Villafranca del Castillo, 1937. (Walter Reuter)

first by one side, then the other. Eventually the Nationalists prevailed, and on 20 July pushed the Republicans back across the Guadarrama river, gaining ground which Miaja's troops would never again recover. (11)

BRUNETE: THE COUNTEROFFENSIVE

The Republican offensive launched on 6 July had been planned as a rapid strike designed to avoid a massive, full-scale clash with the better trained and better equipped Nationalist army. Yet this is precisely what now happened. From 11 July, 60 batteries of artillery and squadrons of German aircraft pummeled Republican positions along the entire front. Between the swirling clouds of acrid smoke and choking dust, the two sides fought over almost every square meter of the parched earth in a grinding war of attrition. The battle raged across the plain—it was no longer possible to determine where exactly the front lay.

The ferocity of the conflict which ensued was recorded in *The Book of the XV Brigade*: "Fierce as had been some of the engagements in which the Brigade had previously participated, those of the following days surpassed them." It was estimated that the Nationalists now had a three to one advantage in terms of aircraft and artillery, and the exposed Republican supply lines were harried continuously: one victim was ambulance driver Julian Bell who was trying to get wounded soldiers to El Escorial (see Chapter 7). One British volunteer recalled:

> Food wagons ran the gamut of aircraft and artillery on the way up to the lines. So too with the water wagons, now more necessary than ever. Rivers marked on maps were dry gullies weeks before the offensive began. The Guadarrama river was available for some days but its brackish waters then dried up. Added to the inevitable, and at Brunete usually accentuated, sufferings of war were the pangs of hunger and thirst in the days of broiling sunshine and nights of clammy heat.

Raging thirst was a torment seared into the collective memory of all combatants. While the Nationalists supply lines generally held up better than their enemies', nobody was guaranteed much-needed water. One Nationalist account told of a Falangist so crazed with thirst that he drank the contents of a beer bottle that had been filled with petrol, only to die writhing in agony before his helpless comrades.

On 18 July the rebels began a counter offensive which not only checked, but now began to roll back, the Republican gains. "Brunete must not fall!" cried Nationalist troops as they fought their way with bayonets fixed through the narrow, rubble-strewn streets of the village. After days of close quarter combat, rebel troops edged back into Brunete on 23 July, while hundreds of Líster's soldiers retreated to the cemetery on the outskirts of the village to the north. Here, on the high ground, they dug improvised defensive positions which they managed to hold in some of the bloodiest skirmishes of

Ruined Brunete, 1937 (Ministerio de Educación, Cultura y Deporte, Archivo General de la Administración [Archivo Rojo])

the entire war. Líster's men cowered in their trenches and sheltered behind the walls of the graveyard, just managing to hold off one Nationalist thrust after another. But now it was the Nationalist high command which became frustrated at their troops' failure to make more rapid progress. Fresh rebel forces were thrown into the sector and, while Líster's exhausted division was finally driven back, some remained in the cemetery to cover the retreat. Of those who stayed, not one survived. It was a telling end to the Republican dream which had begun in Brunete just over two weeks before. (5)

The Soviet advisor reporting back to Moscow on the offensive had little time for such selfless courage, however, and was scathing about the reverse. "Líster's division lost its head and fled," he wrote before adding chillingly, "we managed with great difficulty to bring it back under control and prevent other soldiers fleeing from their units. The toughest measures had to be applied. About 400 of those fleeing were shot." The Polish commander of the International Brigades, Karol Świerczewski (better known as General Walter), reported apologetically to Moscow that there had been an "inexplicable but hasty movement backwards" among the International Brigades too—with the exception of the XI Brigade and the British and American units of the XV Brigade.

*

In the thick of those swept up in the desperate, chaotic retreat from Brunete was a 26-year-old photographer called Gerta Pohorylle, better known as Gerda Taro. German by birth, Taro was arrested by the Gestapo after being caught throwing anti-Nazi leaflets from the roof of a department store near her home in Liepzig. Her Polish-Jewish parents decided that she would be better off elsewhere and sent her to Paris. Clever, multilingual, and pretty, Taro made friends easily—the future German chancellor Willy Brandt and the writer George Orwell were among her Left Bank acquaintances. Money, however, was harder to come by. Under the influence of her lover Robert Capa, a fellow Jewish émigré, she took up photography and started selling her work to magazines, first with him and then alone.

During 1937 Taro made several trips to Spain, vividly recording the war with her small Leica cameras. Capa once said that "if the photograph was not good enough it is because you're not close enough." Taro's extraordinary photographs of those final hours in Brunete, which have only recently come to light, demonstrate that she was prepared to get very close indeed.

On 24 July, a Sunday, Taro was "embedded" with the Republican troops putting up a last ditch attempt to hold Brunete. The commander of the International Brigades in the sector, "General Walter," knew Taro—both came from Polish families—and bawled at her to get out of the battle zone as the rebels advanced. "In five minutes this place will be hell," he shouted, but she ignored him and carried on photographing the mayhem.

Then, along with hundreds of men, tanks, trucks, and

armored cars, Taro was driven back in the Republican retreat along the road north from Brunete to Villanueva de la Cañada. The column was harassed without mercy by swooping Messerschmitts, Heinkels, and Nationalist artillery: one of the German pilots looking down on the scene that day described the destruction as being like "the last day on earth." With men being blown to bits before her eyes, Taro continued clicking her 35mm Leica cameras to record everything that she could, reckless as to her own safety. Perhaps she was suffering from survivor syndrome, well documented among war photographers who come to believe that they are invincible as long as they have a camera in hand. Or perhaps she did not care anymore. Just days before she had told the British journalist Claud Cockburn about "an absurd feeling that somehow it is unfair to still be alive given all the fine people we know who have been killed in Brunete."

When the film ran out in mid-afternoon, Taro and her companion, a Canadian journalist called Ted Allen, decided to try and make their way to El Escorial some 20 kilometers north—a Republican base and safe haven from the shelling. From there she hoped to cadge a lift back to Madrid in time to catch a flight back to Paris the next day, where she planned to rejoin Capa. As they approached Villanueva de la Cañada, Taro and Allen stopped to help a Scottish doctor who was assisting a wounded soldier. The man's legs had been mangled to pulp and they lifted him onto a passing T-26 tank and clambered aboard themselves. The tank carried them to a field hospital by the side of the road to El Escorial about 1.5 kilometers north of Villanueva de la Cañada. Taro helped the man into the dressing station and then saw an open top black car full of more wounded men heading up the road to El Escorial. (12)

The driver pulled over. Taro threw her equipment onto the front seat and jumped onto the running board. The car moved off with a jolt, one within a chaotic convoy of vehicles picking their way north along the shell-holed road. Exhausted, covered in dust and her own sweat, Taro was relieved to be moving. Tomorrow she would head back to Paris where *Ce Soir* newspaper would publish her latest pictures from the war in Spain. Then the strafing from the air began. German Heinkel He 111s spotted the column and began to shoot it up. In the turmoil, a Russian tank in the convoy lost control and rammed the open top car. Taro was thrown from the running board and under the tracks of the tank which split her stomach wide open. She was taken to the English hospital in El Escorial where she died in the early hours of 26 July.

Gerda Taro was immediately lionized by the political left, which effectively organized a state funeral. Hundreds of government and military officials filed past her coffin in Madrid and Valencia. When the cortege arrived in Paris, tens of thousands more turned out for her funeral. Her body was buried at the Père-Lachaise cemetery by the wall where the Communards were executed in 1871, under a tombstone designed by Giacometti.

*

From 27 July 1937 the battle around Brunete began to descend into a war of attrition, a stalemate which continued in the sector until the end of the overall conflict in March 1939. The Republican reverses might have become a rout but, having put a definitive break on the Republican offensive threatening Madrid, General Franco was now eager to resume the rebel push in the north of Spain. Over the summer Nationalist forces were redeployed away from the Brunete front, and they resumed their assault on Santander. The conquest of this strategically important sea port, which the offensive at Brunete had been intended to save, was, in the event, staved off for just a few weeks. By the end of August 1937 Santander was in Nationalist hands.

In 1938 *The Book of the XV Brigade* celebrated Brunete as "a turning point in the war in Spain." It probably was, but not in the way intended. The Brigade record lauds the considerable territory gained, including "a considerable number of highly fortified fascist positions of importance in future operations" and the great advances made by the Republican army in terms of training, discipline, equipment, and staff work, revealing at the same the weaknesses still existing especially in the coordination of various services.

In fact, whatever the gains made, the cost in terms of human life was terrible. Oliver Law, George Nathan, Gerda Taro, and Julian Bell are just some of the names now most remembered among the thousands of casualties. In terms of materiel too, the offensive was a real blow to the Republic, which saw about 80 percent of its armored vehicles destroyed along with a third of the airforce. The Nationalist army had been severely bloodied, too, but less so than the Republicans and, with the aid from Hitler and Mussolini, it was in a much better position to carry on the war. Meanwhile, the Nationalist blockade of Republican-held sea ports was slowly throttling the latter's war effort.

Brunete was the last big offensive on the Madrid front, and the failure triggered a welter of recriminations and doubts in the Republic. According to World War I commander Von Moltke, "no battle plan survives contact with the enemy." Brunete is a textbook example of why the German general may have been right. Despite months of preparation, the Republican commanders failed to anticipate possible problems before putting their offensive plan into practice—and then they had no answers to the Nationalist response when things went wrong. Three Republican weaknesses in particular were exposed on the plain of Brunete. First was the poor caliber military leadership. President Azaña was scathing about communist commanders like *El Campesino,* Líster, and Juan Modesto, who played a leading role in the offensive. With faint praise he damned them as "improvised and without knowledge... they try hard but this does not remedy their incompetence. The only one who knows how to read a map is Modesto. The others not only do not know but don't think it is necessary." When *El Campesino,* for example, was given a map of the front he did not even look at it, but "unfolded it across the table, drawing down, and used it as a table-cloth." And even

Jubilant Nationalists with the remains of a Republican armored vehicle. The loss of military hardware at Brunete was a crippling blow to the Republican war effort. (Ministerio de Educación, Cultura y Deporte, Archivo General de la Administración [Archivo Rojo])

Modesto resented having to work with the regular army. When he was sent a professional officer as his second in command, he refused to speak to the man and threatened to resign unless the officer was withdrawn, which he duly was.

Second, communications between the HQ and what was actually happening on the ground were a shambles. The volunteers from the XV International Brigade complained that "telephone wires, cut several times daily by bombardment, were taped together with bits of cloth and paper, no other material being available." Runners were shot on the open plain. There were few maps so orders, even when received, were not always clearly understood. In short, it seemed as though nothing had been learnt from the Battle of Jarama in February (see Chapter 7). Even when communication lines did hold up, units were not where they were supposed to be—or even where they said they were. Individual commanders were prone to exaggerate success for fear of being branded failures or, worse still, Trotskyist Fifth Columnists, by the communist hierarchy.

Third, Brunete demonstrated better than any other battle to date the importance of air superiority in modern warfare. Within days of the battle's commencement, the Luftwaffe-backed Nationalist squadrons of Junkers, Heinkels, and Fiats were joined by a new German fighter aircraft, the legendary Messerschmitt 109, on some of their first outings in war. Aerial attacks played havoc with the Republican supply lines and units on the ground, which were hopelessly exposed. Antony Beevor observes that that the Republican army spent most of the battle "trapped in a small area on completely exposed terrain," where a prime target were the Soviet supplied T-26 tanks which were knocked out from the air almost at will. Nationalist squadrons ran sortie after sortie from an airfield at Talavera, just half an hour's flying time away, and had a virtual free hit on the Republican force. At any one time there might be up to 200 planes in the air: the effect on ground troops is described by Miles Tomalin, in the poem at the beginning of this chapter.

Another who watched the battle with an unusually keen interest was Colonel Wofram von Richthofen (cousin of the "Red Baron" Manfred von Richthofen), a German advisor to Franco. Von Richthofen reported back to Berlin that Brunete had been a victory for airpower rather than ground troops. The Nazi high command drew its own conclusions. In a couple of years, some of the lessons they learned at Brunete would be put into practice in the skies over London, Coventry, Portsmouth, and other British cities too.

VISITING BRUNETE

The battlefield of Brunete is extensive. Any of the following places can be visited independently or as part of a wider exploration of the battlefield.

ROUTE NOTES

(1) A panoramic view of the battlefield—much as it was then—can be seen today.

Remains of a Republican bunker and the plain of Brunete. Madrid is on the horizon, far left. (David Mathieson)

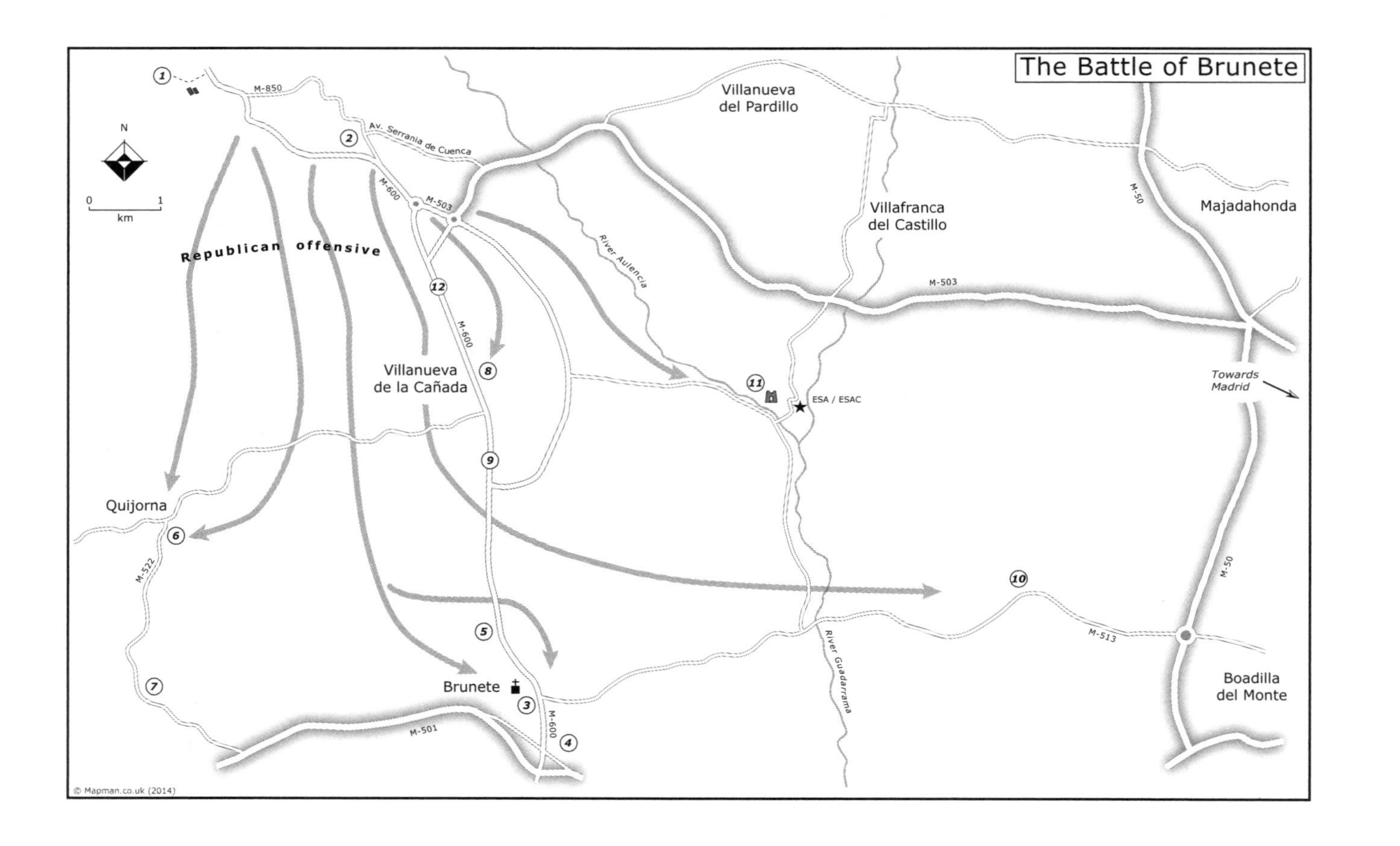
The Battle of Brunete
N
0
1
km
Republican offensive
M-850
Av. Serrania de Cuenca
M-600
M-503
Villanueva
del Pardillo
Villafranca
del Castillo
Majadahonda
M-50
River Aulencia
M-503
Villanueva
de la Cañada
ESA / ESAC
Towards
Madrid
Quijorna
M-522
River Guadarrama
M-513
M-50
Brunete
M-600
M-501
Boadilla
del Monte
1
2
3
4
5
6
7
8
9
10
11
12
© Mapman.co.uk (2014)

Follow the M600 Carretera Brunete towards El Escorial from the roundabout where the M503 meets the M600. Pass the junction with the M850 and remain on the M600 heading north. Some three kilometers uphill from the M600/M503 roundabout is a large sign on the right hand side going up, marked Puente la Sierra. This marks the entrance to an up-market housing estate, and the main entrance onto the estate is called Calle Navarredonda. There is plenty of parking at the entrance to the estate by the security guards' cabin.

Cross over the main M600 between the two red bus stops on either side of the road, from the Puente la Sierra side to the open ground. Take care crossing the road. Follow the footpath which runs from the bus stop onto the open ground, and walk for 300 meters. Directly in front is the Aeroclub Privado with two large blue-gray hangers for light aircraft.

The footpath crosses an unmade road by the Aeroclub. The footpath is marked by two blue waist-high posts. These are signed Red de Sendas: Parque Regional del Curso de Río Guadarrama (Regional Park of the Guadarrama river). Ruta 14 runs between Villa Nueva de la Cañada. Ruta 19 runs between Valdemorillo and Colmenarejo.

The road on the right rises up the sloping ground. Walk along the footpath to the top of this slope (300 meters). The view south now looks over the battlefield. Brunete is on the distant skyline due south. In front is Villanueva de la Cañada (which now largely obscures Brunete). To the left is Villanueva del Pardillo. To the right (but hidden behind the hill) is Quijorna.

Líster's column made their way down from these slopes during the night of 5/6 July on their way to Brunete. The slopes then became part of the Republican defensive line after July 1937. It was heavily bombed, and it is still possible to find occasional debris from the war and shards of shrapnel.

(2) After the offensive of July 1937, the line stabilized and remained largely intact until the end of the war. There are

Republican bunker on the plain of Brunete (David Mathieson)

some well preserved bunkers from the Republican line at the intersection of the M600 and the M850 and Avenida Serrania de Cuenca. These were part of a line of bunkers, some of which can still be seen to either side.

(3) Brunete. Much of the village was flattened to rubble during the war, but the name assumed a mythical status among Nationalists and became a sort of living monument to Franco. Along with other villages in the area, Brunete received special aid after the war under a Francoist program for *las regiones devastadas* (rebuilding devastated areas). Despite this reconstruction and expansion of the village in recent years, there is still much to see from the battle in and around Brunete.

There is normally easy parking in Brunete around the square bordered by Calle de las Olivas and Calle Real de San Sebastián. The center of the village (pedestrianized) is a two-minute walk.

Plaza Mayor. The main square of Brunete is just to the south of the church. On either side of the steps, which lead from the church to the plaza, are plaques. These record the inauguration of the rebuilt village by General Franco in 1947. The inscriptions record: "Esta Plaza Perpetua la Gran Victoria de la Batalla de Brunete en Nuestra gloriosa cruzada de la liberación" ("This square perpetuates the great victory of the battle of Brunete in our glorious crusade of liberation"). Above the town hall on the eastern side of the square, the Falangist symbol of tied sticks is still prominent. There is an ongoing controversy in the town about whether the plaques and symbols should be removed.

The sixteenth-century church of Parroquia Nuestra Señora de la Asunción (Our Lady of the Assumption) is at the corner of the Calle Asunción with the Calle de los Mártires (street of the martyrs—a reference to the Nationalist dead). The church was rebuilt after the war, but much of the original fabric remains and the scars of war are still very visible on the façades, especially to the left of the main door. On the western wall of the church is a well maintained memorial to the Falangist leader José Antonio

Primo de Rivera and other Falangists who died here. The inscription reads: "Caídos Por Dios y Por España" ("Fallen for God and for Spain"). On the southern wall next to the church is another plaque to the Falangist dead.

Brunete's cemetery is by the small roundabout where Calle Madrid joins Camino de los Morales. In the middle of the roundabout is a stone obelisk, which bears an inscription to the Nationalist dead. There is no mention of the Republican fallen.

The Centro Cultural Aniceto Marinas (21 Calle Campo) has in its entrance a scale model of Brunete as it would have been rebuilt with money from the *zonas devastadas* program. The model shows that the new village would have been laid out with a street pattern in the design of a giant basilica. Fortunately (or not, depending on your point of view) the cash ran out, and the grandiose scheme was never completed.

Bunkers are still very much in evidence on either side of Brunete.

(4) Southern bunkers: there are egg-shaped Nationalist machine gun posts on the Camino de Sacedón (at the junction of the M600 with M501). The machine gun posts marked the Nationalist

Remains of an egg-shaped Nationalist bunker at Brunete, with the sierra in the background (David Mathieson)

line of defense on the south side of Brunete. Two are outside 2 Camino de Sacerdón, and another is in the garden of the house (the owner uses it as a wine cellar!). A fourth is in the middle of the roundabout 50 meters up the M600 to the north (towards Brunete). Parallel to Camino de Sacerdón to the east is a Via de Servicio with a Cepsa petrol station. In the fields to the east behind the petrol station are more of the egg-shaped machine gun posts.

(5) Northern Bunkers: there are bunkers at the milestone km 33 on both sides of the M600 from Brunete to Villanueva de la Cañada. Gerda Taro traveled along this road hours before she was killed.

(6) Quijorna: The village was substantially rebuilt after the war, but it is still possible to get a sense of the pre-war ambience. The church of San Juan Evangelista (St. John the Baptist) has been rebuilt and is still on the high ground in the center (rebuilt).

Nationalist bunker at Brunete with the sierra in the background (David Mathieson)

There is a memorial to Falangist dead in front of church, although the inscription and names have faded into obscurity. Perhaps the town council has decided to sidestep controversy by neither removing nor renovating the memorial.

The bar-café El Aguila in 50 Calle Real has a tiled mural of Quijorna after the devastation. It is a friendly place to stop off for a drink and snack.

(7) Bunker: there is a large bunker in a good state of preservation some 3.5 kilometers from Quijorna. Leaving Quijorna on the M522 (known on some maps as the Avenida de San Martín de Valdeiglesias), the road passes over a small bridge spanning the Arroyo de los Morales (frequently dried up). The bunker is on the left-hand side of the road past the bridge

(8) Villanueva de la Cañada: The village of Villanueva de la Cañada has been almost completely rebuilt since the war. The road running through the center is where it was, but the buildings on either side, including the church and town hall, were rebuilt under the "devastated regions" program.

(9) The British Battalion was on either side of the road about 1.5 kilometers outside the center of Villanueva de la Cañada toward Brunete on 6 July.

(10) View of Mosquito Crest. An up-market housing estate called El Bosque has now been built on some of what was Mosquito Crest, and the rising ground approaching it is private land used for hunting (access is only possible with the express permission of the owners). Nevertheless, the rising ground of the crest can be seen easily from surrounding roads and public land. Take the M513 (also marked on some maps as the Calle Río Manzanares) from Brunete to Boadilla del Monte. Cross over the Guadarrama river. Around 2 kilometers from the bridge, in the direction of Boadilla del Monte, is a sign to TCD Installations and a bus stop for the 575 bus (which runs between Boadilla and Brunete). On the left-hand side is a sign

Parque Regional del Curso Medio Río Guadarrama (the area is a protected environment). The Republican forces attempted to push up the rising ground—with the Guadarrama river behind them—on either side of the road. Mosquito Crest is the rising ground beyond the soccer field on the right hand side of the rising road.

(11) Villafranca del Castillo. The solid walls of this fortress were tested almost to the limit by the battle, but are still there today and well worth a visit. The castle is by the European Space Astronomy Centre (signed ESA or ESAC) on the M503 Carretera Majadahonda a Villanueva del Pardillo. Take the exit at km 18 direction *from* Madrid, or exit 19 direction *to* Madrid—the exits are either side of a large red iron bridge which crosses the Guadarrama river. Follow the clearly marked signs to ESA.

Villafranca del Castillo today (David Mathieson)

At the main gates to the center, take the unmade road to the right—the castle is clearly visible—and follow it round for some 300 meters to the rivers Guadarrama and Aulencia. In reality, neither is now much more than a stream, and both are frequently completely dried up.

(12) Gerda Taro was fatally wounded on 24 July on what is the M600, probably about 1.5 kilometers from the center of Villanueva de la Cañada, direction north to El Escorial. Julian Bell, nephew of Virginia Woolf, was also killed on this stretch of the M600.

DELVING DEEPER: TOP TEN BOOKS, TOP TEN WEBSITES

The war in Spain between 1936 and 1939 is one of the most trawled over conflicts in history. In the 1990s it was calculated that some 15,000 books had been published about the war—which works out at roughly 15 for every day of fighting—along with thousands more articles and academic papers, TV series, and documentaries. Many more have been added since then, and (inevitably) there is now even an online war game about the Battle of Jarama. Armed with such a mountain of information, it should be a straightforward task to construct a definitive factual account of what happened where and when. Sadly not. The picture is confused by a lack of basic data, conflicting opinions, and the passage of time; years after he had actually reported on the war from Madrid, the journalist Cyril Connolly quipped that he no longer believed half the stuff he read about the conflict, including much of what he had written himself.

Nevertheless, there have been some excellent attempts to make sense of the evidence and the following list should help the interested traveler to read on.

A Concise History of the the Spanish Civil War by Paul Preston: Fontana Press, 1996

Professor Paul Preston of the London School of Economics remains the doyen of Spanish Civil War historians, combining thorough academic clout with a breezy, readable style. Preston has produced numerous books covering different aspects of twentieth-century Spanish history, which are all worth reading, but for those who want a quick-start introduction this is a gem.

The Battle for Spain: The Spanish Civil War 1936–1939 by Antony Beevor: Penguin, 2006
Military historian Beevor has a different take on the war from Preston's, and is more critical of Republican shortcomings, for example. As a former professional soldier, he also offers lucid insights into the battles themselves and explains why both sides were so often frustrated in their strategies. This book is not just for military buffs though; Beevor has the knack of writing with an eye for the telling anecdote.

Gerda Taro by Irme Schaber and Richard Whelan: Steidl, 2009
This book was produced to accompany a major exhibition of Taro's work in the United States. The clearly written, straightforward articles about her life and technical aspect of her work are richly illustrated with quality reproductions of her photographs from Spain.

The Spanish Civil War: A Very Short Introduction by Helen Graham: Oxford University Press, 2005
At under 200 pages, this bite-sized history is widely considered to be one of the best concise accounts on the war. Like Paul Preston, Graham knows how to combine academic heft with a strong narrative drive. For anyone short on time but looking for a quick history of the conflict which covers all the main events and puts the whole tragic episode into context, this is a very good place to start.

The Book of the XV Brigade: Records of the British, American, Irish and Canadian Volunteers in the XV International Brigade in Spain 1936–38, reprinted by Warren and Pell, Torfaen, 2003
This collection of earthy, vivid, and deeply subjective accounts was produced as a sort of yearbook by the survivors of the XV International Brigade. Most of the short articles are by Brigade members describing what they did and saw. Contributions range

from brassy propaganda to moving introspection: together they provide a fascinating insight into the collective Weltanschauung of the Brigade.

Franco's International Brigades: Adventurers, Fascists and Christian Crusaders in the Spanish Civil War by Christopher Othen: Hurst, 2013
The majority of foreigners who fought in the war did so on the side of the Nationalists—Germans, Italians, and Moroccans being among the most numerous. Yet there was also a mixed bag of Irish, French, and other European fascists who turned up in Spain to take part in Franco's crusade. This lucid book tells their colorful story and greatly helps to put the war into the context of politics in the 1930s.

Britain and the Spanish Civil War by Tom Buchanan: Cambridge University Press, 1997
A must for readers who want to understand more about how the British body politic reacted to the conflict. Nothing was quite as it seemed. Supporters and sceptics of "Non Intervention" were to be found across the political spectrum, while attitudes shifted as the war evolved. Oxford academic Buchanan does an excellent job in tracking the kaleidoscopic trends and in putting them into wider European framework of the time.

Crusade in Spain by Jason Gurney: Faber and Faber, 1974
This bitter-sweet account of the war by a Jarama veteran is told with insight and irony; it is a surprisingly funny book given the subject matter. Multiple failures are spelt out: shambolic organization, Brigade incompetence, and Stalinist cynicism are all there. But this makes the book all the more moving. With more of a shrug than bravado Gurney seems to ask, "what else could we do but fight fascism?"

Hotel Florida: Truth, Love and Death in the Spanish Civil War by Amanda Vaill: Farrar, Straus and Giroux, 2014
Ernest Hemingway and Martha Gellhorn, Robert Capa and Gerda Taro, and Arturo Barea (the head of the foreign press service) and Ilsa Kulcsar (his assistant/lover) were three couples whose lives converged at Madrid's Hotel Florida (many of the characters and the hotel are covered in this book). Rich in anecdotes, Vaill tells the story of Civil War Madrid through their complicated lives, and the result reads like a well-researched novel.

Defence of Madrid by Geoffrey Cox: Ortago University Press, 2007
In the absence of other volunteers from the newsroom, the young Cox was sent by the *News Chronicle* in London to cover what was expected to be the fall of Madrid. He stayed for several months and this book, first published in 1937, fully captures the terror, tensions, and intrigues of living in the city under siege. Later in his career Cox went on to found ITN's flagship news program *News at Ten*, and his journalistic flair for "telling the story" is evident in this book, which is one of the best on the siege of Madrid.

In addition to printed books, there are some very useful websites about the Civil War and International Brigades. In a welcome trend, local groups in Spain are now reclaiming their history and publishing research online. The following list, however, is of the best web pages in English, with just a couple of Spanish sites which have exceptionally good photographic collections.

International Brigades Memorial Trust (IBMT)
http://www.international-brigades.org.uk/
The IBMT was set up to promote the memory of British and Irish volunteers, and its website is the reference point for news, reviews, and much archive material. The site contains a range of information—from events going on around the UK to education packs for students and the merchandise of snazzy IBMT-shirts.

Abraham Lincoln Brigade Archives (ALBA)
http://www.alba-valb.org
ALBA is the main source of information about the American volunteers. The database, organized in conjunction with New York University's Tamiment Library, is impressive: an A-Z list of biographies of the "Lincolns" and digitalized archives of documents and sound recordings (click on "resources" to access). There is also a complete archive of the Brigade's magazine *The Volunteer*, which is still going strong.

Imperial War Museum
www.iwm.org.uk
This superb website has rich seams dedicated to the Spanish Civil War and the International Brigades (use the internal search engine to find them). The digital archive contains hundreds of documents, photographs, and sound recordings which help to bring the story to life. Access is free—a real bargain.

Spartacus
http://spartacus-educational.com/Spanish-Civil-War.htm
Encyclopedic is the only word to describe the Spanish Civil War section of this educational website. Thousands of entries provide a comprehensive database: biographies of participants and observers, political organizations, military structures, battle plans, timelines, and explanations of the issues involved are just

some of the categories on offer. Not bedtime reading perhaps, but very clearly presented and great for fact checking.

Asociación de Amigos de las Brigadas Internacionales (AABI)
www.brigadasinternacionales.org
With a small office in Madrid and a dedicated group of volunteers, the AABI organizes events, discussions, and campaigns in Spain to promote the memory of the International Brigades. The website is constantly updated with information about upcoming activities. The site has an English version and is worth checking out if you are on a trip to Madrid—in the spirit of the group, foreigners are made very welcome!

Foro Social de la Sierra de Guadarrama (Social Forum of the Sierra of Guadarrama)
http://www.forosocialsierra.org/
Foro is a network of groups which seek to protect the environment and promote activities in the mountains of the Sierra de Guadarrama just outside Madrid. A click on the Fotos de la Guerra (war photos) link opens an impressive gallery of images taken around Guadarrama and El Escorial between 1936 and 1939. There is no English translation, but the photographs speak for themselves.

Richard Baxell
http://www.richardbaxell.info/
Academic, author, and trustee of the International Brigades Memorial Trust, Richard Baxell runs one of the liveliest Civil War blogs. The site abounds with the latest book reviews, upcoming events, and general tit-bits of research unearthed by Baxell or fellow historians. Not surprisingly, a well-plugged book on the site is Baxell's own latest called *Unlikely Warriors: The British in the Spanish Civil War and the Struggle Against Fascism.* And why not? It's a very good read.

www.thespanishcivilwar.com
This lively website is a veritable cornucopia of information—photos, maps, documents, and events—about all aspects of the Civil War. The founder, Nick Lloyd, has lived in Barcelona for more than two decades and also runs a successful walking tour company about the conflict in the city.

Porta de la Historia
www.pdlhistoria.wordpress.com
Despite the title, this website is all in English. The PdlH banner proclaims that it is a site "for those who wish to explore the Spanish civil war," and this it does via a plethora of fascinating video clips, testaments, and research. With regular updates, the site is fresh and vibrant.

Spanish Sites Battlefield Tours around Madrid
www.spanishsites.org
The author's own web page—and embryonic version of this book. For the past three years Spanishsites has organized tours of the battlefields around Madrid; clients have included student groups, relatives of IB volunteers, politicians, journalists, diplomats, and a host of visitors to Madrid with an interest in the war. Visit the site to book your own bespoke battlefield tour with Dr. David Mathieson.

ACKNOWLEDGMENTS

Much of this book was written in Argüelles, the *barrio* or district of central Madrid which has been our family home now for more than 15 years. In November 1936 a column of the International Brigades marched down our street on its way to the trenches of Parque del Oeste, less than two minutes away, while the building in which we live was badly shelled by Nationalist batteries sited in the Casa de Campo. I sometimes wonder what happened to the people who lived in our apartment 80 years ago and try to imagine how the park must have looked during the war. These, I thought, were personal obsessions until a neighbor confessed that he hardly ever walked in Parque del Oeste without reflecting on the same things. It was a reassuring confirmation that I was not alone in my musings, and over the years many local people have shared experiences, facts, and titbits with me about the war; to friends, neighbors, and especially my companions from the local Moncloa-Aravaca branch of the PSOE I am grateful for the stimulation and encouragement to find out more and write this book.

Some of the conversations which have provided material for the text were painful. Being with relatives of the victims of the post-war repression when they met at the small cemetery in San Lorenzo de El Escorial, for example, helped me understand more but it was difficult to listen and must have been even more so to speak. I am particularly grateful to José Manuel G. Carrizo, who with immense dignity showed me family memorabilia and led me through details about the life and death of his father, Vicente, whose story is told in Chapter 7.

Apart from conversations, this book is based on extensive

reading and research in archives. The librarians in the Faculties of Architecture and Philosophy in the Complutense University and at the Spanish National Library in Madrid, especially the head photographic archivist Isabel Ortega, were most helpful. In the UK, staff at the Imperial War Museum—and the online access to their digital archives—could not have been more user-friendly. Other staff at the Marx Memorial Library, the People's History Museum, the Working Class Library, and the Lewisham Local History Society have also helped me search for some needles in otherwise impenetrable haystacks. Professor Nigel Townson from the Complutense University in Madrid lent me a library of books to fill in the many gaps in my knowledge.

International Brigades' organizations supported the research too. The Asociación de los Amigos de los Brigadistas Internacionales and its Director, Severiano (Seve) Montero, have been enormously helpful. Seve was one of the first people with whom I ever discussed the idea of this book, and he has been a source of encouragement ever since. Jim Jump at the International Brigades Memorial Trust in London dealt patiently with a plethora of questions. Two other Madrid-based organizations whose volunteer members are dedicated to researching the Civil War have been invaluable sources of information: GEFREMA and the Asociación TAJAR. Ricardo Castellano, from the Colectivo Guadarrama, who has an encyclopedic knowledge of the fortifications around Madrid, and local historian Jesús Vázquez Ortega helped to tie down many of the loose ends in the chapter on Guadarrama. My understanding about what happened at Brunete was greatly enhanced by Ernesto Viñas, who took me around Mosquito Crest. Gregorio (Goyo) Salcedo did the same at Jarama: no trip to the Jarama valley is complete without a stop at the Mesón El Cid bar-restaurant to see the unique museum which Goyo and the owner Pilar have established there. Hely Reuter kindly gave permission to use the photograph taken by her father Walter Reuter, which appears on p.205.

It has been a privilege to share this knowledge with visitors to Spanishsites.org, the project which I established a couple of years ago to explore the battlefields of Madrid. Talking while we walked, many visitors have shared their extensive reading and insights with me, and these conversations have been immensely helpful in focusing this book. I am also deeply indebted to Dr. Mercedes Jiménez Palop and Dr. Frank Jürgensen, whose skill and care have allowed me to keep walking when my arthritic joints might otherwise have given up.

Steve Brown, Victoria Hughes, and my editor James Ferguson all did a great job trawling though the text to weed out embarrassing errors, and those that remain are all my responsibility. In addition, many friends have helped explore the routes, suggested improvements—or simply tried to help me make sense of it all over a *caña* or two. I owe special thanks to the staff and students of Salem International College (especially Dr. Günther Klause), Niki Avgerhinos, Rosie van de Beek, Tom Burns Marañon, Paul Davies, Mike Dwyer, Ian Gibson, Chris Hale, Michael Harris, Carlos Hidalgo, Mikkel Larsen, Nick Lloyd, Joyce MacNeil, Cameron Marshall, Belen Montes, Miguel Salvatierra, Andy Pollock, and Alan Warren.

The biggest thanks of all, however, are due to my wife Emma Leakey and our children Olivia and Ermias. I know I have tested their patience to the limit: there must have been times when they felt that the entire XV International Brigade had taken over our house. Yet they have supported this project throughout and without them nothing would have been possible.

Finally, lest anyone think I have written this book in the belief that war is some sort of Boy's Own adventure, I don't. I am the first Mathieson in three generations who has not had to fight in Europe. My grandfather fought with the British Army in the World War I, and my father with the RAF in World War II. They were both proud of what they did—as I am of them—but neither left me in any doubt that war is a wretched, not a glorious, affair. I am truly grateful to them for that insight and that I have never had to fight in a war myself.

Argüelles, Madrid, September 2014

INDEX

Albacete 20, 31
Alfonso XIII, King 5, 36, 44, 78, 176
Anarchists 3, 5, 6, 10, 15, 38, 53, 63, 84, 94
Aragon 20, 101
Army of Africa 7, 23, 76, 79, 113, 122
Asador Alto del León (bar-restaurant) 164, 165 (map)
Assault Guards 6, 7, 43, 68, 72
Asturian miners 6, 48, 96
Attlee, Clement 24
Azaña, Manuel 26, 36, 54, 59, 175-176, 183, 185, 192, 211

Badajoz 31, 79, 86
Baedeker guides 25
Barcelona 2, 6, 19, 27, 38, 160, 187, 230
Bell, Julian 55, 178-180, 183, 206, 211, 223
Bergson, Henry 55
Boadilla del Monte 199-201, 215 (map) 221-222
Brandt, Willy 208
Brecht, Bertolt 150
Browne, Felicia 24
Brunete 15, 20, 178, 185-203, 205-211, 213-223, 215 (map)
Buckley, Henry 47, 189
Buñuel, Luis 3, 55

Calvo Sotelo, José 6, 7
Canary Islands 7, 62
Capdevielle, Juana 89-90, 99, 111
Carrizo, Vicente 180-182
Casa de Campo 10, 11, 13, 33, 40, 46, 48, 73-74, 76-78, 81-85, 87, 96, 99, 102-103 (map), 104-107, 109, 114
Casa Paco (bar) 107
Casablanca (Rick Blaine), 25
Castillo, José 6, 41, 43-44, 157
Castillo, Enrique 157-159
Castillo de Villafranca 204, 215 (map), 222
Catholic Church 2, 3, 9, 21, 23, 69, 169, 174-175
Charlesworth, Albert 21, 123
Chicote bar 32 (map), 47
Churches
  Nustra Señora de la Asunción (Brunete) 218-219, 221
  San Juan Evangelista (Quijorna) 220
  San Fernando (Madrid) 32 (map), 53-54, 70
  Villnueva de la Cañada 196-197, 221
Communists 5-6, 10, 15, 21-22, 24, 26-28, 30, 37, 39, 40, 50, 52-53, 63, 69-71, 81, 99, 117, 120, 131, 135, 159, 162, 178, 189-190, 194, 203, 211, 213
Condor Legion 8, 23, 123
Conservative Party (UK) 20, 22
Copeman, Fred 29, 129-131, 196, 198
Cornford, John 49, 55, 76-77, 89, 95, 97-99, 104, 111
Cox, Geoffrey vii, 47, 49, 159, 194, 227
Churchill, Winston 8, 26, 47
Churchill, Peter 180
Curie, Marie 55

"Dad's Army" (Home Guard) 28
Dalí, Salvador 3, 55
Delaprée, Louis, 35, 43, 49-50
Democratic Party (USA) 21
Donnelly, Charlie 55, 141
Durruti, Buenaventura 38

Einstein, Albert 55
El Escorial, San Lorenzo150-151, 153, 169, 171, 173-177, 179-184, 196, 203, 206, 209-210, 216, 223, 229

Falange 3, 6, 171, 176
Fanjúl General Joaquín 64, 66, 70, 72
Fascism vii, 3, 8, 21, 28, 30-31, 39, 81, 99, 140, 161, 203, 226, 229
Flynn, Errol 25
France vii, 25, 26, 27, 135, 183, 188
Franco, Francisco vii, 3, 6, 7-10, 13-16, 19, 21- 23, 28, 31, 35-37, 39, 40, 43, 53, 54, 56-58, 61-62, 76-77, 79-80, 88, 92, 95-97, 101, 104, 107, 110, 112-115, 120, 131, 135, 140, 151, 158, 168, 169-173, 176-177, 182-183, 186, 189, 194, 210, 214, 218, 226

Gálicz, János 118, 199
Gellhorn, Martha 25, 141, 152, 227
Germany 8, 15, 28, 138, 171, 187
González, Valentín (*el Campesino*) 159, 194
Guadarrama *sierra* 13, 58, 60, 65, 74, 77, 90, 113, 118, 129, 150-160, 162, 164-166, 168-169, 173-174, 177-178, 183,
Guadarrama river 199-200, 204-206, 216, 221-223, 226
Gurney, Jason 30, 118, 123, 126, 131-133, 135, 147, 203, 226
Gropius, Walter 55

Heath, Edward 22,
Hemingway, Ernest 13, 24, 47, 50, 52, 100, 109, 120, 141, 150-153, 157, 159, 161-163, 165, 169, 171, 173, 175, 177, 179, 181, 183, 227
Hitler, Adolf vii, 2, 8, 23, 28, 79, 171, 186, 211
Hugo, Victor 11

Ibárruri, Dolores (*La Pasionaria*) 27, 189
International Brigades vii, 9, 17, 31, 33, 35, 44, 47-49, 51, 77, 82, 84, 89, 90, 97, 102, 104, 107, 110, 112-113, 115, 118, 132, 138, 142, 144, 146-148, 154, 180, 186, 194, 196-198, 200-2004, 208, 213, 225-229
  American Lincoln (and Irish) 18, 20, 24, 28, 138, 140-142, 146-147, 197, 200-201, 202-204, 229, 225
  British (and Irish) 9, 20, 21, 24, 28, 33, 99, 112, 115-118, 120, 123-139, 142, 144, 146-147, 196-200, 202-203, 206, 208, 221, 225, 228, 229
  French-Belgian 18, 19, 97, 115, 120, 124, 127, 129, 138, 147
International Brigades memorial, London 20
Italy/Italians 2, 3, 8, 14, 18, 23, 28, 82, 114, 135, 161, 174, 201, 226

Jarama, Battle of 13, 20, 26, 112-149, 145 (map), 196, 200, 203, 213, 224, 226
Jones, Jack 24
Jones, John "Bosco" 123, 139

Keynes, John Maynard 55

Labour Party (UK) 21, 24, 29, 130
La Mancha 20, 154
Law, Oliver 203-204, 211
Le Corbusier, 55
Lee, Laurie 24, 154
Líster, Enrique 159, 190, 191, 206, 207, 211, 216
Lucáks, Pavol 25

Madrid
  Atocha 31-32 (map), 33, 44, 33, 40-41, 82
  Bar Miami 32 (map), 49
  Campamento 65, 75
  Capitol Cinema 32 (map) 52
  Carabanchel 13, 65, 75
  Casa Labra 32 (map) 43
  Círculo de Bellas Artes (Bellas Artes

building) 32 (map), 39, 40, 58
Ferraz (calle) 65, 68, 74, 103 (map)
Fuencarral (calle) 6, 32 (map), 43-44
Fuente de Cabestreros 32 (map) 53-54
Gran Vía 32 (map), 33, 44, 46-50, 52-53, 82
Hotel Florida (Plaza Callao) 32 (map) 50-51, 152, 227
Hotel Gran Vía 32 (map) 47-48
Hotel Ritz 32 (map) 36, 38
Luisa Fernanda (calle) 68, 70
Miami bar 32 (map), 49
Cárcel Modelo (Model Prison) 72, 87, 108
Palacio Real (Royal Palace) 32 (map), 58, 75, 106
Parque del Oeste 12-13, 33, 40, 58, 60, 74, 76-78, 82-83, 87, 93-95, 99-100, 102-103 (map), 105-107, 109
Plaza de España 11, 33, 58, 65-66, 68, 74, 83, 87, 93 107
Plaza Mayor 32 (map), 58
Prado Museum 32 (map), 36
Princesa (calle de la) 33, 83, 103 (map)
Puerta del Sol 9, 32 (map), 33, 41, 43, 93
Reina Sofía Museum 32(map), 33, 35, 39
Residencia de Estudiantes 32 (map), 55, 57-58
Telefónica Building 32 (map), 44, 46, 47, 49, 152
Templo Debod 74, 104
University city or *Ciudad Universitaria* (Chapter 5), 11, 12, 22, 26, 33, 49, 56-57, 76-77, 83, 87-88, 90-91, 93-99, 101-103 (map), 104, 109, 110, 111
Usera 13
Manzanares river 11, 68,77,81-82, 84-85, 87, 90, 93, 103 (map), 106, 109, 110
Merriman, Robert 140, 141
Miaja, General José 10, 80-81, 94, 114, 196, 205
Militia (Republican) 10, 14, 39-41, 53, 63, 65-72, 81-82, 84, 88, 92, 94, 151-152, 154, 155, 157-159, 183, 188
Mola, Emilio 13, 41, 65, 70, 75, 113, 153-154, 182
Montaña Barracks 7, 60-73, 75, 76, 87, 93, 113, 153
Morata de Tajuña, 117-118, 130, 136, 138, 142, 144, 145 (map), 146, 148-149
Mesón El Cid and Museum 146, 149
Mosquito Crest 199-201, 204, 221-222
Millán Astray, General José 56
Mussolini, Benito vii, 2, 8, 23, 88, 135, 161, 171, 186, 211

Nazis 2, 15, 20, 26, 29, 34, 45, 107, 138, 172, 176, 182-183, 187, 194, 208, 214
Nathan, George 202, 203, 211
Neruda, Pablo 33, 107
Non-Intervention Agreement 8, 21, 25, 26, 83, 226

Orwell, George 17, 24, 30, 208

Paracuellos 73, 181
Pasarela de la muerte 91, 92, 109
Picasso, Pablo (and *Guernika*) 3, 33, 34, 36, 39
Pozas, General Sebastián 80, 114
Primo de Rivera, General Miguel 1, 5, 88
Primo de Rivera, José Antonio 38, 40, 170, 176, 219
Puente de los Franceses 82, 85-87, 91, 106, 108-109
Pyrenees 15, 44, 183
Robertson Justice, James 24

Robeson, Paul 24
Ryan, Frank 138-139

Quijorna 190-195, 199, 215 (map), 216, 220-221

Rodríguez Lozano, Captain Juan 66
Rojo, Colonel Vicente 9, 10, 81, 85, 94, 100, 114, 115
Romanillos Heights 196, 199-200
Russia (USSR) 8, 37, 39, 50, 51, 52, 90, 114, 120, 136, 140, 187, 189, 203, 210

Sanjurjo, General José (and *sanjurada*) 6
Stalin 8, 22, 37, 39, 84, 120, 187, 194
Stern, Manfred (*General Kléber*) 83-84
Stravinsky, Igor 55
Swierczewski, Karol (*General Walter*) 208

Taro, Gerda 178,186-187, 208-211, 220, 223, 225, 227
Tito (Joseph Brotz) 21
Trotskyists 10, 213

Unamuno, Miguel de 56-57

Valle de los Caídos 150, 162, 168-174
Varela, General José Enrique 10, 11, 13, 84, 85, 86, 114
Villanueva de la Cañada 178, 190, 192, 195-197, 199, 200, 204, 209, 215 (map), 216, 220-223
Villanueva del Pardillo 204, 215 (map), 216, 222

Winteringham, Tom 28, 29, 117, 118, 120, 121, 124, 125, 126, 132, 133, 135, 136

Yagüe, General Juan 80, 86

Zapatero, José Luís Rodríguez 67